Me

re GILETTE

Me?re Gilette. [A tale.] By the author of

Me

re GILETTE

Me?re Gilette. [A tale.] By the author of

ISBN/EAN: 9783741157943

Manufactured in Europe, USA, Canada, Australia, Japa

Cover: Foto ©Andreas Hilbeck / pixelio.de

Manufactured and distributed by brebook publishing software (www.brebook.com)

Me

re GILETTE

Me?re Gilette. [A tale.] By the author of

MÈRE GILETTE.

BY THE AUTHOR OF

"An Old Marquise," etc., etc.

LONDON:

18 WEST SQUARE, S.E.

Depôt: 21 Westminster Bridge Road, S.E.

1893.

Dedication.

TO
LADY HERBERT OF LEA
THIS SIMPLE STORY,
THE SCENE OF WHICH IS LAID
NOT MANY MILES
FROM PEACEFUL BOURY,
IS DEDICATED:
A SLIGHT RETURN FOR MANY
ACTS OF KINDNESS.

MÈRE GILETTE.

CHAPTER I.

It was summer in the old Norman village where Mère Gilette lived with her son Jean. Jean was nineteen years of age, and he was all that was left to her now; but if he were spared, she would say sometimes, then she would be content. She forgot, I think, that there are things worse than death.

Jean was the youngest of six. He was the only one who had lived to grow up. Little Claude-Marie had been the one who came nearest to doing so, having died on his tenth birthday, but then no one in the village had ever expected Claude to grow up. "When they are like that, the good God takes them home early," the old women had been wont to say, after watching the boy in his scarlet and lace robes, serving the Mass of Monsieur le Curé, while the sunlight fell through the stained windows on the fair young head, as the lad knelt with clasped hands, gazing up to where the white Christ hung above the altar. Claude-Marie had served the Mass on the day he died, and then he had gone out in the fields to labour, for it was the time of harvest. And about the hour of noon, just when the Angelus was pealing from the old grey tower, the boy had fallen prone upon the ground, and in a few hours he was gone. A doctor came and spoke of sunstroke, but Mère Gilette did not care for science. The Lord of the harvest had seen her Claude-Marie was ripe for heaven—that was all. They robed the fair white body of the boy in his acolyte's dress, and bore him away up the village street to the quiet graveyard where his father and brothers slept, and the Mère Gilette walked behind, and little Jean with her.

It was nine years and more since that bright day in the harvest-time when the sorrowful procession had gone in at the gate of God's-acre, and little Jean was little no longer, but had grown tall and strong, and, what was more, was said to be engaged to Babette Rison, the only daughter of a rich neighbouring farmer. Jean was apprenticed to the village blacksmith, and laboured away lustily all the long day through: in the evening he was content to sit on the bridge, beneath which the swift river ran, and smoke his pipe with Gaspard and François, and the other young fellows whom he had known all his life. And when the stars were out, and lights were gleaming from under the eaves of many a little cottage, they went into the *café* and drank long draughts of simple Norman cider, and then went quietly home to bed long before the clock in the church steeple had chimed eleven.

And then there were Sundays, when, very early, long before Jean was awake, Mère Gilette would creep down the tiny staircase, and out and away to where the doors of God's house stood wide open. And there she would kneel at the sanctuary-rails, close to the spot where her Claude-Marie used to kneel in the long-gone days, and with a faithful few would receive Him whom Monsieur le Curé brought them in the golden ciborium. And by and by, when the sun was high in the heavens, she would come back again for *Grande Messe,* leaning on her Jean's strong arm; and under the grey arches of the dark old Norman church she would thank *le bon Dieu* for all His mercies, and tell herself that if her son were but spared, then would she never be sad or downcast any more. She forgot, I say, that there are things worse than death: it seemed to her that that was the great evil which threatened all her treasures. Five of her children, and the husband of her choice, lay beneath the tangled grass and the yellow *immortelle* wreaths in the churchyard, where in the still summer evenings she went to pray. She did not know that there were mothers who envied her her dead children, though there are many like that. Such a one I knew once. "Look you," she would say sometimes, "that poor soul weeps for her first-born, and I—I envy her!"

Yes, those were happy days which the Mère Gilette spent while her son laboured in the blacksmith's-shop, or sat on the bridge smoking his pipe. Oftentimes she did not see him between sunrise and the hour when he returned home to stretch himself on the pallet in his quaint little chamber under the eaves, but she did not mind. He was close at hand. If she took the trouble to walk down the steep street and cross the bridge, beneath which the silent river flowed, there, in the blacksmith's shop, under the shadow of the buttresses of the grey sanctuary, she would find him. She knew he was happy and doing his work. She herself was always busy.

The Mère Gilette rose very early. Sometimes in summer, two hours before the Angelus sounded, she would creep down the tiny staircase into the common sitting-room, with its broad hearth, and its great oak presses filled with the rich white linen which had been part of her bridal dower. And there she would set to work, cleaning and scrubbing and polishing till there was not a speck of dust or rust to be seen anywhere, and one might have eaten one's dinner off the very floor. And then she would set the window and door wide open, and let in the beautiful fresh summer air, while on the stone hearth the embers smouldered and the coffee-pot simmered, and the sunlight danced on the sacred pictures which ornamented the whitewashed walls. It danced, too, on the little Calvary which her piety had erected in a corner of the room, and which, in the long-gone days, in the *Mois de Marie*, little Claude had loved to decorate with wild flowers. He had fairer flowers to gladden his eyes now, she would think often, as she rested for a few minutes from her daily toil.

And then Jean would come clattering downstairs and away to his work, and the Mère Gilette would take up her rosary and start off to church—to church, where another boy, clad in the familiar scarlet and lace, lighted the candles and served the Mass of Monsieur le Curé now. Mère Gilette did not think the lad moved about the sanctuary with the quiet reverence of her little son; but she strove to put that idea from her, thinking it lacked charity. And after the Mass was over, Mère Gilette would go home once more, and continue the scrubbing and polishing till it was time to cook the eggs, or the beans, or whatever it was which made up the simple mid-day meal. But in the afternoon the widow did no work—at least, no hard work. In winter-time she would sit by the fire on the hearth, and in summer on her doorstep, while her brown hands plied the bright knitting-needles, and now and then she paused to tell a decade of her rosary, or to exchange a greeting with a neighbour.

But once or twice a week there was no knitting, and any stranger coming to see Mère Gilette might knock and knock, for the little cottage was tightly barred up, and every one who heard the sound knew that the owner had gone down the village street, through the quiet lane, past the mill with its drowsy, sleep-compelling sound of machinery at work, past the crumbling walls half covered with ivy and moss, and in through the iron gates, up the avenue of limes, to the old *château*. Madame la Duchesse de Mérillac lived at the *château*, and long ago, before her own marriage, Mère Gilette had lived with her as one of her maids. Then the great house had been bright and cheerful, while gay bevies of ladies strolled in the gardens, and parties of blue-coated sportsmen rode down the avenues on their way to hunt in the forest.

But now all was still and silent, and half the windows of the old place were kept closed, and the courteous host slept with his fathers beneath the shadow of the cross: and Madame la Duchesse?—Madame la Duchesse de Mérillac, in her long, black robes, paced slowly up and down the deserted, grass-grown walks. The *château* had always been rather sombre since the death of the last Duke, but it was only about three years since the great, intense stillness settled on it which reigns there always now. That was the day on which Mdlle. Laure, the Duchesse's only and beautiful daughter, died of consumption, within a few weeks of her twenty-second birthday. Up and down, up and down the deserted gravel walks, for two long hours every afternoon, winter and summer alike, the black-robed figure moved. It was very lonely, very sad, but—but it was better than sitting still. Yes, I think so, too, with Madame la Duchesse.

It was when she returned from these solitary walks that the owner of the *château* would be told that the Mère Gilette desired to speak with her. And then, in the small circular sitting-room opening out of the great drawing-room—which was never used now—the lady would find her old servant, and the pair would chat away together for an hour and more—chat of the days when Mdlle. Laure had lived, and how the deserted corridors of the *château* used to echo once with the sound of the child's gay laugh, as she and her cousins chased each other from room to room. And sometimes—in summer seated under the tall trees of the quaint, stately garden, or in winter by the wood-fire in the turret chamber—they would speak of later times, of weary, sleepless nights, and grievous thirst and coughing, and of how uncomplainingly she bore it all; and as she spoke, the eyes of Madame la Duchesse would wander round the room till they fell upon the picture in the large morocco frame, and she saw again the wavy brown hair and sweet grey eyes of her dear dead daughter.

But they did not speak all the time of Mdlle. Laure, for though the heart of the Duchesse was well-nigh broken, though all the gladness of her life seemed gone from her to return no more, still she was not selfish. "Come," she would say often to her old servant, "come, *mon amie*, thou hast given time enough to my grief; tell me now of thy little Claude-Marie, and of the days when there were many of you in the cottage down yonder."

At first it had been an effort, a grievous, weary effort, to say it, and she had felt then almost callous to the sufferings of others, but it was different after awhile. Monsieur le Curé had said always it would be so. Madame la Duchesse liked to hear of little Claude-Marie very much indeed at last.

"Thou art happy in having thy son at home, so near to thee," Madame said, one June evening when Mère Gilette had been paying rather a longer visit than usual, and the warning bell for Madame's solitary dinner was even then sounding from one of the turrets of the *château*. "Thou art happy, I say."

"Yes, I am thankful," the peasant woman answered; "but, Madame will forgive—but the good God, He knows what is best for each one of us. It is for a wise reason that Madame is alone. All He does is for the best."

"Yes, I doubt it not," looking away to where the dying sunlight streamed through the green trees on the right of the *château*. "Once when they used to say that, it seemed *impossible*—that was when my darling was leaving me, three years ago now. I remember it was Monsignor himself who came from Beauvais to say it to me, and I thought it could not be true, but I know now that he was right. It was very early in the morning—just about the sunrise—the day after she had received the last sacraments, and we thought the end nearer than it was, and he said almost what you said then, and I cried out, 'O, no, no; it cannot be for the best—it *cannot.*' And he just raised his hand and blessed me, and said, 'Poor soul, poor soul; by and by—by and by. God's grace must have time to work, like everything else.' I have learned to say it now, at least"—smiling faintly—"I *hope* so."

Then Madame la Duchesse turned and went back into the room where the dead girl's picture stood—back into the quiet, deserted *château,* and the Mère Gilette went onward down the green avenue. She was thinking—thinking how happy she was not to have been left quite alone in the world, but to have her son always near her—to be able to feel and know that he was alive, and safe and well. Poor Madame la Duchesse!

Then the Mère Gilette closed the great iron gate behind her, and went slowly along the familiar lane to the village. If she had known then that before many days had come and gone she would almost envy the lady of the *château* in her solitude—if she had known, I say!

CHAPTER II.

THE clock in the church steeple was striking seven as the Mère Gilette reached the familiar stone bridge. She looked round, half expecting to see her Jean smoking his pipe, but he was nowhere about. In the distance, on the other side of the stream, she could see that the doors of the blacksmith's forge were tight shut. Evidently the work of the day was over. She stood still, looking down at the swift flowing river, enjoying the cool sound of the water against the stonework of the arches.

Presently footsteps made her look up. It was Monsieur le Curé himself, coming slowly along with a thoughtful expression on his calm face. He was not handsome, Monsieur le Curé, having a sallow countenance and raven black hair; but his eyes had a far away look in them which told of something better than mere beauty of face, and his smile was sweetness itself. He took off his hat to the peasant woman. Mère Gilette and the good priest were firm friends.

"It is a beautiful evening," he said. "I am going down towards the green. Have you heard there is a meeting there? Some people have come from Paris to tell us many wonderful things. I suppose"—looking round at the deserted little *place* near at hand—"I suppose that is where all the world has betaken itself. Are you looking for your Jean, my good friend? Ah, no doubt he has gone too, to hear the eloquence of those strangers. The young love always what is fresh."

He was only forty himself, but youth seemed to him a long way off. To hear always of sin—of those who had forgotten God, perhaps that was what had done it. To him it seemed so. He could not bear to have his Christ neglected thus—it cut him to the heart. He wanted his flock, all of them, young and old, weak and strong, to love Him even as he himself loved. As he walked along the quiet lanes around that Norman village, his lips moved in prayer that it might be so before he died. He was always thinking of it.

"The young love always what is new," he said again with his sad smile.

"Monsieur le Curé speaks truly," the widow answered. "It were better perhaps if it were otherwise."

"Ah!" Monsieur le Curé did not commit himself, but in his heart he thought that the woman was right. Then he bowed again and prepared to pass on.

"If Monsieur le Curé should see my Jean, would Monsieur be kind enough to say I am gone home? He knows that I went to the *château* at five, and I said as I passed the forge that I might be a little late—if Monsieur would be so good."

"I will tell Jean," the black-robed figure said, and went onward down the lane which led on to the Green.

It was very still that summer evening: scarcely a sound broke the stillness, save when now and then there came the clack of wooden sabots in the distant street, or else in the distance the far-off thunder rolled. A storm was passing along the line of hills at the back of the *château*: it had been threatening for the last two hours. Very likely it would break over the village later in the evening. It had seemed all day as if something were going to happen. Then the priest came out on to the green. There was a crowd a little way off, listening to some speaker. He would go and listen too, he thought. Then he came to the edge of the throng, and there was an outburst of cheering.

"What is it for?" he asked an old man, near.

"For the *Révolution sociale* which is coming," was the answer. He was a stranger to the Curé.

"For the *Révolution sociale!* What is that?" he asked.

"The time when all priests, aristocrats, and tyrants shall meet with their deserts," was the insolent answer.

"And their deserts—what are they?"

The Curé was not clever. His mind moved slowly unless—unless it was about *That* which is over everything.

"Death," returned the other fiercely, thrusting his face close to that of the priest. He was a big ugly man, and he smelt of brandy, and altogether he was not pleasant. The Curé drew back just a little. The man thought he was afraid, and drew nearer. The priest, as I have said, was not clever, but he understood quickly enough then, and smiled.

"Death?" he exclaimed, "that is not much! Perhaps if you had seen him as often as I have, you would not think to frighten us from our work with threats like that."

The man addressed looked surprised. It was the thing of all others which terrified him the most—that grim king. He hated all tyrants, and who was such a tyrant as death? But he was ready enough to invoke his aid against those who opposed him. It was only for *himself* that he was afraid. A little knot of people gathered round the pair. They were tired of listening to the anarchist on the platform who was inveighing against royalty. So long as he had spoken of the way to obtain the wealth of others it had been all very well, but royalty—they did not know very much about it. A prince of the house of France lived not twenty kilometres off, and gave employment far and wide to those around his beauteous home, and once, when there had been cholera in the south, had gone to visit the poor sufferers there; while the hired head of the Republic, "whose own the sheep were not," had stayed safe at home! They were not quite sure that royalty was such a bad thing after all.

"If you had seen him as often as I have, you would not think to frighten us from our duty with threats like that," the Curé said again.

"Seen him often—ah, yes, but that is when he comes for others—those poor ones whom you send forth to their eternal sleep with threats of a false hell," was the sneering answer. "When he comes for you—this death whom science has not yet destroyed—then we shall see if you are as brave as you say; above all if he comes for you in the shape of the knife of a guillotine."

"The guillotine!" the Curé laughed aloud as he repeated the word. "That is an old acquaintance. And yet I do not think he has ever made much impression. He was at work very often during the years which followed the announcing of the principles of 1793, and we priests had many of us the honour of following in the footsteps of royal martyrs. Did you ever hear what was said the day after the massacre at the abbey? They said—one of them, I forget now his name, but he was one of your great men— that he was amazed, overwhelmed, because those wearers of the *soutane* had gone to meet death as though it were but a bridal-feast. No, the guillotine will not do, my friend. You must find something else if you want to frighten us— something more terrible than death. Death?" looking away to where the sun was sinking down in the far west, making, by contrast, the black thunder-clouds look blacker than ever: "Death is only another name for the gate of life."

There was a little silence. The groups which had gathered round the pair looked from the priest to the communist. They wanted to know what the latter would say next.

"Well," he answered after a pause, "perhaps after all the guillotine is not so very dreadful. I have often thought that it was too merciful a death for you priests. Perhaps," an evil smile lighting up his face, "perhaps by the time the Revolution comes, we shall have found one more suitable to you. Your words are very brave, but that is only because you are well and strong; if he came, that death of whom we speak, if he came close, and put out his hand to take you, I wonder if you would be brave then."

"I hope so, I trust so. Long ago, monsieur, soon after I was ordained, when I first came here, and was *vicaire* to our late Curé, I saw him very close indeed. That was an unhealthy year, and there was much want. In the autumn, typhus fever came, and we were busy always in the *Maison Dieu*. We were hard worked then, and it seemed as if the only time we got any fresh air at all was at the funerals in the afternoon. Monsignor had to send us help, for both Monsieur le Curé and myself fell sick of the disease, for it was of a very infectious type. I do not think, monsieur, that I was afraid, though I was so far gone that they thought it necessary to give me the last sacraments. Our good Curé died of it. I remember that they told me afterwards that one evening, near the end, he asked how long he had to live, and they told him that he would probably last till dawn. He wept a little then. He would not see God that night as he had hoped, he said. Death, you see," smiling a little, and very sweetly, "Death had not much terror for this Curé, monsieur."

There was a murmur of admiration among the group. They were not quite certain which was right, many of them. Sometimes they thought one thing, and sometimes another, but just then their sympathies were with the priest. It seemed a grand thing, this creed of his, which could rob the dread of their lives of half his terrors. There was a little murmur as though they would say that he, this Curé, had spoken well.

The communist heard it, and an evil look came on his face. He began to speak, but his voice was drowned in a burst of applause. The meeting was about to break up, and a final resolution had been carried to the effect that it was desirable for the public good that all capitalists should be put to death. Then in the general enthusiasm there was a sudden movement, and the little group at the outskirts of the crowd was broken up. Perhaps the communist and hater of priests was not sorry.

The Curé walked slowly away across the green on his way back to the village. He scarcely noticed the people who passed him, he was thinking so deeply. His heart was sad. He could not understand why men should hate them thus when they desired only their welfare here and hereafter. Then he looked away at the dark thunder-clouds, and remembered that it had been so long ago, and that *He* had said it would be so with those that came after. "Ye shall be hated of all men for My Name's sake." It was fitting that as a disciple he should comprehend something of the sufferings of his Divine Master. Then he crossed the bridge and saw the doors of the church were still open, and went in.

It was very dark inside the great Norman church. As he passed along the silent nave he looked up at the arches overhead, and then at the dim, dying light coming in through the rich stained windows. "I have loved, O Lord, the beauty of Thy House, the place where Thy glory dwells. One thing I have asked of the Lord, that I may dwell in the courts of His House all the days of my life," he murmured to himself. Then he went onward, past the High Altar with its great crucifix, past the shrine of the Blessed Mother, illuminated by the light of two or three waxen tapers, onward to an altar before which a solitary lamp was lighted. Then he knelt down, and covered his face. He was in the presence of the Holy of Holies.

The night had fallen, and the *De profundis* was sounding from the belfry, when the Curé again lifted the heavy matting, and stepped forth into the still summer air. In the distance he could hear the water lapping against the arches of the bridge, even above the tramp and laughter of some young men who were passing the doors of God's sanctuary. By the light of an oil lamp suspended across the street he saw that most of them were strangers to him, with the exception of Jean Gilette and another young man. He stood back a little way to let them pass, when suddenly he remembered the Mère Gilette's request, and called to the former, "Jean!"

The passers-by started a little. They had not noticed the black-robed priest standing under the grey arch, and were laughing at some filthy witticism which had been spoken by one of their number. In the silence which reigned around, the good priest caught the last words. He stepped forth then. He was a little man, small of stature, and thin from fasting and long vigils, but they fell back before him.

For a moment all was silent. Then he spoke, and the light flashed from his dark eyes, and his voice rang forth loud and clear as he rebuked them for their words spoken before the open door of God's House. Then he turned to Jean. Within a stone's throw of where they stood, his cousins lived. Their windows were open, and they might have heard. Did he not know that it was a man's duty to protect the women of his blood from insult? The scorn that rang through every tone of his voice was like the lash of a whip.

"Who are these whom you are with?" he asked. He did not know their faces.

"They are strangers from a neighbouring town," Jean answered sulkily. "They have come over to support the lecturer who has been speaking to the people of the district."

"To support the lecturer!" the priest repeated. "I can well believe it. I saw your good mother awhile ago, she bade me tell you that she had gone home. She feared you might think she would be remaining late at the house of Madame la Duchesse."

"Madame la Duchesse!" echoed one of Jean's companions. "For my part, if I had my way, his citoyenne and all like her should very soon sneeze in the sack."

The Curé turned his black eyes on the speaker, and laughed a little, just as one does sometimes when one is weary with disposing of some oft-put and absurd argument.

"Death," he said, "that is your *one* threat for those who differ from you. He frightens you so much yourselves, that you do not understand how one may have little fear of him. This lady of whom we speak, do you think she dreads it—she who is a widow, and weeps always for the loss of an only child?"

The men did not answer. They went away in silence, drawing young Jean along with them.

. . . .

"Thou wast late last night, my son," the Mère Gilette said the next morning. "I heard thy step long after the clock struck two. That is why thou art behind thy time this morning. If thou dost not hurry, thou wilt be late for thy good master."

She turned from the hearth as she spoke the above words, and looked at her son as he stood with heavy eyes, waiting for his cup of coffee.

"Master!" he echoed contemptuously. "Yes, he is *that*, but if things were fairer, he and I would be equal. Why should he have money and I none?"

"Because thou art young, and he has worked for it all his life," Mère Gilette answered. "If thou followest in the footsteps of good M. Turquin, thou wilt be well off some day."

"Some day!" cried the young fellow. "Yes, perhaps—only *perhaps;* and that, when I am too old to enjoy it!"

Jean went away after that, muttering to himself.

"The lad speaks strangely to-day," Mère Gillette thought as she watched him with anxious eyes. "Pray God he fall not into evil ways."

There was a cloud upon the face of the good woman as she knelt before the altar in the parish church during the Mass of the good Curé. "Pray God he fall not into evil ways," she said again and again, and resolved to keep watchful eyes upon the youth. Then her glance fell upon the tall, slender figure of Madame la Duchesse de Mérillac in her deep mourning, where she knelt, holding her prayer-book with one hand, while the other rested on the sill of the now vacant *prie-dieu* beside her. Madame la Duchesse loved to feel that her hand was resting *just* where her Laure's hands had been. Sometimes when she came into the church at noon and found she was alone, she would kneel and kiss the place. A great longing was with her always to see again the sweet grey eyes, and the wavy brown hair with which she had loved to play.

"Poor Madame la Duchesse!" Mère Gilette thought, as she saw the gloved hand wandering to its customary place. "Poor Madame la Duchesse! To be quite alone—to have laid her only child in the grave!" She did not know then that she would live almost to envy the bereaved mother her dead one.

"You do not get on very fast this morning," Turquin, the blacksmith, observed, as he watched his assistant lazily preparing a shoe for the furnace. "I think you cannot be well."

"I am well enough," the young man answered roughly.

"Perhaps something is wrong in his love affair," the blacksmith thought with a smile. He remembered the days when a hitch had come regarding his own marriage with his Fanchette. Fanchette had been a village beauty, and her family had looked higher than one of the men at the forge, nevertheless, honest Turquin had had his way in the end, and she had now been his wife for thirty years.

"Look up, Jean," he said cheerily, as he passed out to his mid-day meal, leaving the young man in charge. "Girls are coy at times, but if you be in earnest, you will win the day!" Fanchette had been a little backward and doubtful at first, but the stout blacksmith had won her at last, solely by the weight of his great love.

"Girls!" echoed the young man, "I was not thinking of them. It is too early for me to think of marriage yet, even though I am betrothed. They say, too, that marriage is an invention of the priests—that it should not be binding. Why should one not take a wife as one takes a house, on trial or for so many years?"

It was fortunate that the blacksmith had passed out of range of such remarks, or it is possible he might have resented his assistant's views rather warmly, for Turquin was hot-tempered at times.

"There is something wrong, certainly, in his love affair," the blacksmith said to himself at the hour of closing, as he looked round and saw how little young Gilette had accomplished in the course of the day. "Something must be wrong," and Turquin was lenient in consequence, and did not say more than that he hoped they should get through a good bit of work the next day.

That evening there was another meeting on the green, and the same lecturer spoke. There were not quite so many people present as at the previous one, but it was more harmonious. A resolution was passed that all the churches ought to be turned to secular uses at once, and another to the effect that all property should be equally divided. Then the lecturer started back on foot for a neighbouring town near some large mining works, and some of the crowd accompanied him part of the way cheering for the Social Revolution, and the one who cheered the loudest was

Jean. As they went by the walls of the *château* grounds, they tore some of the ivy from the crumbling stones, and trampled it under foot. There were many in the crowd who had benefited by the good deeds of the Duchesse de Mérillac, but their minds had been poisoned by the lecturer. She was an aristocrat, that was sufficient.

CHAPTER III.

THE summer days passed quietly along in the still Norman village, and the time of harvest came. In the fields the men toiled at gathering in the golden corn, and the young folk would go out and meet them returning from labour at the sunset hour. The Mère Gilette could hear them singing, long before their footsteps were audible in the quiet street. She would sit on her doorstep with the eternal knitttng in her hand, pausing from her work now and then to tell a chaplet of her rosary, or to say some pleasant word to the passers-by, but she never stayed to see the harvesters coming back. The last time she had done that was the night before her little Claude-Marie died when he had been one of the gay throng.

She could see him now, bursting into the little cottage, with a great bundle of the rich golden corn, which the good farmer had let him take because he wanted to make gay his little shrine for the feast of the great Mother of God, which would fall in two days' time. She could see the sun-burnt hands placing the sheaves in the white china vases among the tapers close to the image of the Blessed Mother, and near to where the white Christ hung. Claude-Marie had kept the feast when it came—Mère Gilette was sure of that—but he had kept it with the angels. The faded wisps of corn stood in the china vases yet, all dead and withered, but she could not make up her mind to take them away from where the boy's brown hands had placed them long ago.

So when the harvesters came trooping noisily by, the Mère Gilette would steal into her cottage, and kneel before the shrine, and look at the dead corn and whisper a prayer as she did so, for the soul of her little Claude-Marie.

"Thou art all alone, good friend," Turquin, the blacksmith, said one evening, entering the little cottage as the *De profundis* was sounding. The people were out walking in the fields in the light of the glorious harvest moon, and the village street was very quiet.

The Mère Gilette did not answer for a moment. It seemed to her that trouble was coming. She had felt it hanging over her for many days past, and her heart was always beating quickly, as though in anticipation of some evil. She has just time to whisper a prayer that, if so be that it should please Him, she might be spared the drinking yet again the chalice of woe—that chalice which is given so often by the Man of Sorrows to His best beloved.

"Yes, I am alone," she said at last. "I often am now. Sometimes I do not see Jean for two or three days at a time."

The great blacksmith shook his head sadly.

"It is of him I am come to speak," he said at last, and then the Mère Gilette understood that the Master would have her drink of His cup. Well, He would give her strength. Had He not promised so, and when did His promise ever fail? She stood up to hear what the visitor had to tell. It was better so. Had not the Mother of Sorrows stood at the foot of the Cross?

"Yes?" she said a little faintly.

"He is not doing well," the blacksmith went on. "He is late in coming to work, and while he is at the forge he does but little. Last week he was absent for a whole day without leave."

The Mère Gilette bowed her head. She could not speak. It had come, this thing which she had dreaded so, this thing which she had feared through the days and nights past.

"He has got among evil companions. I hear, too, he spends his Sundays over at ——," Turquin named a mining village, about nineteen kilometres distant. "There is much atheism and communism there. It is an evil place. I hear, too, that they are about to increase the works, and more men are coming. They are a rough lot. It will bring bad characters into the place."

Mère Gilette shook her head. "I have heard talk of it somewhere," she said. "M. le Curé told me the Bishop is much distressed at it, but who can prevent it?"

"No one," the blacksmith answered, and then sat silent, as though unable to make up his mind to speak.

"You bring me some evil news, I know," Mère Gilette said at last. "Tell me what it is."

"Thou art right, good friend," the blacksmith answered. "It is this. Out of regard for thee —for the sake of old acquaintance, and because I and my wife have liked the boy, I have borne much lately—ill temper, idleness, oaths, and even——" Turquin paused. He could not find it in him to wound this mother's heart, even to justify himself.

"And?" she said at last, hoarsely.

"And!" echoed the blacksmith, "is that not enough without an 'and'? But he is young, and faults of youth are——"

"There is something else you were about to add," the Mère Gilette broke in. "Tell me; it is better to know all."

"It was foolish of me to let slip what there was no need to say. Have no fear about that; the lad has no real taste for strong drink, but once or twice lately, when he has been in the company of some I could name, he has had a drop too much."

The good blacksmith did not seem to think the offence so very terrible, but with his listener it was different. She gave a little cry, and put out her hand, as though to keep off this blow. And yet—yet, before the blacksmith spoke she had known! Twice lately she had guessed that it was so—guessed, as in the grey light of dawn she had heard the heavy footsteps pausing on the narrow wooden stairs. She had not gone out, had fought against her fear, had hoped against hope, and now, her hope had failed her. She gave a little cry, I say. Her dead husband's son! her Claude-Marie's brother!

"He is young, good friend, he is young," the honest blacksmith said. "It is not of an occasional slip like that I think so much. Lads do it, now and again, because they think it *manly*, and as I said awhile back, he has no real taste for drink. No, it is these new-fangled ideas I dread, which are making him idle and full of discontent. I have spoken without avail. It is a thousand pities. I hear a whisper of it all has reached the ears of the father of his betrothed, and that he is wrath. I should grieve if that were broken off, for such a wife would be the making of the young fellow. She is a gentle, good girl, this daughter of old Rison. Perhaps if M. le Curé spoke, or better still Madame la Duchesse at the *château.*"

Mère Gilette paused before she replied. "He avoids M. le Curé now," she said at length, "but if Madame would condescend. It is a good idea. I thank thee, my old friend. I will go to the *château* to-morrow. Then, if I can make an excuse to send him there, Madame might speak."

The blacksmith rose. "I grieve for thee," he said simply. "Fanchette grieves too. I had meant to tell the lad to-morrow that he must seek some other place, but I will give him another trial. He does no work now, and I must take on another hand. It will be a trifle out of my pocket, but it is a sacrifice I make gladly for thy sake."

Mère Gilette tried to tell him of her thanks, and failed. The great blacksmith wiped the moisture from his handsome grey eyes, and turning, went out into the quiet village street and the pale silvery moonlight.

"Turquin!"

The blacksmith had gone a pace or two, but

he stopped and came back when the Mère Gilette called him.

"Yes."

"Do not tell anything to others about the lad. You say already a whisper has reached M. Rison's ears. I would that he should hear no more of it. My friend, it is not because it is a good match from a worldly point for him that I desire it, for Babette's dower will be large, very large, but as you say she is good, she will lead him on to better things. I love the girl right well, but I tremble at what you say. At the best of times M. Rison never really approved of the proposed match."

"I will be silent as the grave," the blacksmith said, and went away.

And the Mère Gilette knelt down before the faded wisps of corn, knelt on far into the night, the only light in the little chamber being that of the tiny oil lamp which burnt on the little shrine, and threw its rays on the white limbs of the dead Christ who hung upon His Cross.

And that night Jean came not home at all. The Mère Gilette never closed her eyes. When the clock chimed five, and the bells of the church began to peal, she went out into the sweet fresh summer air, and stole in through the west door into the old Norman church, and waited patiently till M. le Curé came out in his white vestments and, bearing the golden chalice, made his way to the altar of the Mother of God to say his morning Mass.

"It is a good thought," the priest said, as he disrobed in the sacristy, and the Mère Gilette whispered to him the blacksmith's idea concerning Madame de Mérillac, while the old sacristan bustled about and arranged the vestments for M. le Vicaire, who would say the seven o'clock Mass.

Mère Gilette went home, and made clean and bright the little cottage, and prepared the coffee, but Jean did not come. An hour before noon she could bear it no longer, and made her way across the stone bridge to the forge. The blacksmith saw her coming, and went out to speak to her.

"Is Jean here?" was all the white lips could ask.

"Yes. But do not enter. He is best left to himself. We have had some words. I tried my hand again, and failed. Very likely it was my fault. I am hasty, and speak too sharply. If it had been Fanchette now—she might have done some good, but as for me——" The blacksmith broke off, and shook his head. He had a profound belief in his wife's good sense; indeed, folks said he attributed to the lady many qualities which she did not possess, but then is not love blind?

Mère Gilette tried to tell him that she appreciated his goodness, but failed. Words do not come easily to all when the heart is full. The blacksmith nodded, and turned back to his work once more, while the good woman made her way out of the village street, along the quiet lane, till she came to the ivy-covered walls, and the rusty, coronet-crowned gates.

Madame la Duchesse was sitting out on the west terrace, her dead child's favourite dog lying asleep at her feet, and in her hands her Book of Hours. She looked up and smiled when she saw who it was—smiled sweetly, sadly, as she ever did now—and then suddenly the light died out of her face, and she stood up.

"Some trouble has befallen you," she said in her hushed, gentle voice. "Speak, *mon amie*, and if I can be of service, I will," and she laid her hand on the arm of her old servant.

"Yes, Madame was right," Mère Gilette said, "and trouble had come. She spoke in confidence. She did not wish all the world to know it yet—they would know it fast enough she feared—but Jean had fallen among evil companions. The boy was young and at present easily led. M. le Curé understood all, but the lad avoided him now, and he turned a deaf ear to his good master's warnings. If she could contrive that he should come with some parcel or message to the *château*, it might be, perhaps, that Madame would condescend to speak gently to him?"

"Yes, I will do so," Madame answered; "but is it wise? The young love not to be reproved, and, though I knew Jean very well when he was a little boy, I seldom see him now. Still if you wish it?"

"Madame is good. I desire it much," Mère Gilette answered.

"Then send him here to look at the horses' hoofs: who knows but what they require new shoes," Madame de Mérillac said, with her sad smile.

"Is my son here?" Mère Gilette asked at the door of the forge on her way home, that warm August day.

"Yes, he was there," the blacksmith answered, and called, "Jean," who came forth from the interior, rubbing his heavy eyes, and looking very much as if he had been fast asleep, instead of being hard at work at his master's business.

"It is thy mother, Jean, who would speak with thee," Turquin said, and moved away, so that he might not be in the way if mother and son desired to talk privately. Mère Gilette stopped him.

"It is only on a matter of business I am come,"

she said, with a little smile. "I was at the *château* just now, and Madame desired that Jean might be sent up to look at the horses' hoofs—that is all."

"You can go now, if you like," Turquin answered. "I will manage by myself for a while. Take a bag of tools with you. There is no knowing but what you may require them, and it is a pity to have to make two journeys to the *château* instead of one."

Jean obeyed, not very readily. One would have thought that he would have been glad of the walk in that glorious August sunshine, but he had been asleep in a dark corner, and would have rejoiced to go back and go to sleep again and try and get rid of the effects of last night's imprudence, for his head ached.

It was two o'clock. The stillness which reigned in the long narrow street was almost as great as that of night. The *persiennes* were closed in all the houses, and trade in the small shops seemed at a standstill, and Jean's footsteps were the only sounds which broke the silence.

Jean went slowly along, past the mill and along the road bordered on the right by the ivy-covered walls of the *château* grounds. There was a little *café* on the left, just before you came to the iron gates, and Jean turned in and had a cup of coffee, for he thought that might make his head less heavy. Then he went on up to the stables, and began to examine the hoofs of the horses. In less than a quarter of an hour he had finished all that he had to do, and was just preparing to leave the stables, when the coachman called to him: "Jean."

"Yes."

"Madame desires to speak with thee. She is seated round by the turret."

The blood mounted to the young fellow's face. In the old days, when he was younger, to come to the *château* and see Madame la Duchesse had been to him a great event, but that was long ago. He had drunk in eagerly the poison of the lecturer's words. Why should *he* wait on Madame—should *she* not rather come to *him*—he who was one of the sovereign people? He would have liked to give utterance to his thoughts, only somehow he lacked the courage to do so. He was not very big, and the coachman of Madame la Duchesse was almost as muscular as Turquin. He held his peace, and moved slowly round to the other side of the *château*.

CHAPTER IV.

"It is long since I have seen you, Jean," Madame de Mérillac said, looking up from her work at the young fellow who stood in front of her, blushing and awkward. "Once you were wont to come very often. I can see you now with your hand in that of your good mother, coming up yonder avenue." The lady gave a little smile as she spoke. It seemed to her so strange that this great, broad youth should be the tiny little toddler that she recollected so well. Then the smile faded away. She had remembered that in those old days her Laure had been beside her, clinging to her and laughing. Almost it seemed that she could *hear* that laugh. Surely no child had ever been so beautiful as hers. Then her eyes fell again on Jean, and she thought of the purpose for which she had sent for him. She must not be selfish. There would be time enough by and by to conjure up dead visions of the past. For the present it was enough that she should think only of the anxiety of her faithful servant.

"We are old friends, Jean, you and I," Madame said, looking up at him again with her gentle, kindly smile. "You will not take amiss a word of warning? We old folk, who have been through the world, and have bought our experience, are able now and again to put a little of the wisdom we have acquired before our young friends. If they would but listen! But alas! it is seldom that they do. It is only when it is too late that they understand. 'If I had but attended when you spoke; but now!' It is always thus in the end."

The lady paused, and glanced at the young man. Jean fidgeted uneasily. He did not know what to answer. The colour mounted to his face, and in his heart was a fierce anger against his mother. It was she of course who had been to the *château* to complain of him. He stood there fingering his cap, not knowing what to say. He would like to have carried out the principles which he had heard enunciated by the lecturer on the green, but he was afraid. She looked so grand, so stately, this lady before him. And yet she was very simply dressed, wearing nothing but the deepest and plainest mourning. Madame Blondel, the wife of M. Blondel, the great mine-owner who owned a large *château* in the village, dressed in silks and satins, yet she did not look like Madame de Mérillac. He would have said just what he chose to that fat Madame Blondel, but before the quiet, stately form of the Duchess, he was silent. He murmured something about the horses, and believing they were as well shod as any horses in the world ; but he was a poor hand at fencing that day, and his answer lacked skill. Across the face of Madame de Mérillac there came a little look of contempt. She liked what was open and true.

"I am not speaking of the horses, and I think you know that very well," she answered. "It is of yourself I speak, Jean, of yourself and the anxiety that is in the heart of your good mother."

"Of what is it that she complains?" he asked uneasily. He did not know yet how much Madame knew. It was necessary that he should find that out, he thought, before committing himself to a reply.

"It is not alone your mother who complains, Jean," the lady made answer. "Good Turquin finds his work neglected. And then, M. le Curé: I hear that you have become a stranger to him."

Jean tried to rally himself a little. "M. le Curé!" he said with a laugh. "Madame must be aware that when one grows up one's ideas change on these subjects. As a child it is all very well—one believes what one is told, but when one becomes a man, one requires something more."

"And this question of religion—of the truths of Christianity—have you studied it very deeply, my good Jean?" Madame asked. There was a little sarcasm in the tone of her voice. She did not mean it, but it was there, and the young man noticed it. The hot blood mounted to his face, and his anger gave him courage.

"I cannot say that I myself have studied the matter," he answered, "but I have spoken and listened to those who have. These things that our priests preach are but fairy tales. For old women like my mother it is all very well—it helps them to bear the troubles of life—but we know that it is all false."

"We *know!*" Madame echoed his words in surprise, then she gave a little laugh. "My good Jean," she went on, after a moment's pause, "I will not be angry with you. But do you know, *mon ami*, that you have disposed of a few people whose judgment is worth perhaps a little more than that of the lecturers on the green? It seems to me that such names as Messieurs de Chateaubriand, de Montalembert, Lacordaire, de Ravignan, Darboy, and a few others that I could mention, are at least worthy of respect. They are men of this century who have lived but for Christianity. I do not think that you can very well say that you 'know' to be false what they believed. I think, if you pause to reflect, you will see that it is a little foolish to speak like that."

Jean did not answer. The quiet tone of superior wisdom in which Madame de Mérillac spoke, angered him, but yet he did not reply. He felt that perhaps it was more prudent on his part to be silent, lest he should expose his ignorance. But he would not give in.

"I know that I believe nothing that M. le Curé does," Jean answered roughly. "As for these other gentlemen of whom Madame speaks, that is all very well. They can believe what they like as long as they do not ask me to share their faith."

Madame de Mérillac shook her head.

"Poor Jean!" she said. "You do not know what you say. That was His plea for each one of us on Calvary. We all need it. You are strong and well, and to-day death seems a great way off. I have heard in my visits to the poor in Paris many sentiments similar to yours, until one day the dark figure appeared to beckon them away. And then—'O, send in haste for M. le Curé!' Poor, despised M. le Curé! Ah, what a change! But we are drifting, my friend. I sent for you to speak, not on religious topics, but as to your behaviour to your good mother,

Jean; she has toiled for you and she has seen many sorrows. You are all that she has left. Will you bring her grey hairs in sorrow to the grave?"

The young man was silent.

"And then the work? That should be done with all your heart. Turquin is a generous master. He has no son, and in a few years when he retires, you might set up for yourself. Work when you are young and strong, and then by and bye will come honourable repose. Turquin himself was in just the same position as you, my good Jean, when he began life, and see what a comfortable house he has now, and how well-to-do he is. Come, will you not give me a promise, Jean, a promise for the sake of our old friendship, to attend no more of these lectures—to go home and be a good son to the best of mothers, and to work hard at the forge once more? And then is there not a little sweetheart? Some day you will bring her home a bride if you labour hard, and your life is honourable."

The young man was silent for a moment. In his heart he knew that he had been far happier in the old days when he had laboured sturdily in Turquin's workshop, and had given an arm to his mother on Sundays when the bells were pealing for Mass. Then he remembered what the lecturer had said, and reflected how grand it was to be independent, to have no fetters at all, to do in fact just what one liked. Why should he care for this Madame la Duchesse? How was she any better than himself? Was he not one of the sovereign people? Why should Madame sit, and he stand?

He put on his hat, and answered insolently, "Certainly I shall make no such promise. I can well understand why you wish me to hear no more lectures. You know very well that it is there we are taught our rights—our power—there that we learn that we are your equals, and not your slaves, as you would have us believe. For hundreds of years you ground us down, starved us, ill-treated us; but those days are over. It is only lately that I have learned all this. And let me tell you this: there is a day coming when we shall mete it all back to you—when we shall administer to you your deserts. If you want your horses shod, get Turquin to come for the future. I am not servile enough for you. You sit there, and keep me standing! It is rather I who should sit, and you, citoyenne, who should——"

Madame de Mérillac rose. Her face had grown white, and in her eyes was a look of amazement. It was the first time in all her life that she had received an insult. She had been born a daughter of the great house of Chatériot, and all the grand blood of her race rose against this hewer of wood and drawer of water who dared to speak thus to her. "Leave my presence —at once," she said.

And, awe-struck, Jean obeyed. As he went down the avenue of limes he knew so well, he wondered when next he would see the face of Madame la Duchesse!

For a while after she had been left, Madame de Mérillac stood motionless. She could scarcely believe that the young man whom she had known from his babyhood, the son of her old and faithful servant, had offered her such an insult. How dared he! How dared he! Then she stopped. She had been insulted, yes but then, had not Some One greater than herself also received outrages?

"God and kings drink deep of the cup of insult offered to them by the children of men," she murmured, unconsciously quoting from a great writer. She had been guilty of pride. Perhaps had she been more gentle she might have won the young man round. She would go to where she might learn to be gentle, to the house of her God. She went away through the gardens, across a field or two, and then came out through a private gate into a little open space above the bridge. A few paces further brought her to the door of the church. She lifted the matting, and entered.

It was cool and pleasant in the church that summer afternoon. The light came in through the rich stained windows, and fell here and there in hues of crimson, blue, and yellow. The place was deserted, and Madame's footfall, soft though it was, seemed to echo under the vaulted roof. She passed up the long aisle, crossed in front of the high altar where the tall candlesticks towered aloft, onward to the chapel of the Blessed Sacrament. She drew a chair near to the rails, and kneeling down, covered her face with her hands.

It was long before Madame de Mérillac moved. She knelt on while the bells in the tower kept pealing quarter after quarter. It is not easy to subdue pride. Even after years of weary conflict, when we think that at last we have made some progress, lo! something unforeseen occurs, and we find that the demon is there seemingly as powerful as ever. By and bye, the soothing influence of prayer began to tell. She raised her head and gazed long and earnestly up to where the white Christ hung above the altar. The wound-prints in His sacred Hands were made because of her. This thought sufficed. The conflict was over. No anger was in her breast now when she thought of Jean. She was only sorry that she had not pleaded further. Her faithful servant's son! Surely nothing that she could do would be too much for any one belonging to her, for had not Mère Gilette been with her in the days of sorrow? She would try and see Jean again, try yet once more to win him back to better ways. Then Madame rose, and went out into the summer sunlight. As she passed back along the Norman nave, she saw M. le Curé in his white cotta and purple stole sitting in front of his confessional, with his breviary open on his knee.

"Hoping for some strayed sheep," he said with a tired smile, as Madame passed. That was his one thought, to bring back those that had erred to his Christ. For this M. le Curé spent his life.

It was very warm out there in the narrow street which ran parallel to the Grande Rue, but Madame de Mérillac went on her way quietly. As a rule, she did not start for the cemetery till six o'clock while the weather was warm, and it was only striking the half after four as she came out of the church, but poor Jean had upset her usual routine. She went up the hill, along the narrow lane to the city of the quiet dead. Madame passed among the many graves till she came to where her Laure was sleeping. A simple marble crucifix marked the spot, while to the right lay the girl's father beneath a grey stone slab richly carved with the coronet and arms of the house of Mérillac. Madame knelt down in turn beside the resting-places of her dear dead.

It was long before she could make up her mind to come away. She knew they were not *really* there, but yet somehow she seemed closer to them among the green mounds and wooden crosses than elsewhere. By and by she rose, and with gentle touch rearranged the flowers on her dead child's grave, and then passed through the chief gate, down the steep Grande Rue to the house where the Mère Gilette lived. She knocked twice but could get no reply. The good soul must be out, she thought, and turning the handle went softly in. The little white-washed room was deserted. Madame sat down, and gazed at the little shrine and the faded wisps of corn.

The time wore on. Madame would not have waited, only she felt uneasy. She could hear the quarters chiming. By and by the Angelus sounded, and still she sat on. It was just seven when the latch was lifted, and the Mère Gilette entered. Madame gave a little exclamation, and rose. She saw by the white, drawn face of her faithful servant that grief had come upon her.

"Sit down, sit down," she said. "*Mon amie*, I fear evil has befallen thee." And she took hold of the peasant woman's rough hands, and drew her gently into a chair.

Mère Gilette sat without speaking where she had been placed, rocking herself to and fro, and now and then giving a piteous little moan, as one does in grievous pain.

"Poor soul, poor soul!" Madame la Duchesse said, and that was all. When it is like that, it is better to be almost silent. In sorrow so deep many words seem only to chafe.

At last after a long while, the Mère Gilette grew a little calmer. She moistened her lips and looked up at the kind, gracious face bending over her.

"I ask Madame's pardon," she said a little faintly. "He was the last of them all, and now he is gone, and I—I am alone."

"Gone!" Madame echoed. "Jean gone!"

Mère Gilette bowed.

"He went to see you, Madame, at your direction. I hoped so much from this interview. I thought perhaps it might change his conduct. I could not rest till I had seen him, and I walked back towards the *château* and met him returning. Alas, it had failed. I ask your pardon for his insults to you. I rebuked him sternly, for the first time in my life. I know that I was harsh to him. He was wrath that I had spoken to you, and he left me and I came home. *Mon Dieu*, I had thought I had known wretchedness enough for this day, but it was not so. After a while he came here—Jean came. He was like a madman. M. Rison had been to the forge, had forbidden the engagement, had told him that he should never speak to Babette again. He thought that it was my doing—*my* doing! I who would have cut off my right hand to save him one minute's pain. He said—no, there is no need to repeat it. When they are young and like that, they do not know what they say. Enough that he has left me swearing that he would look upon my face no more because I had parted him from Babette. I did not understand. Since then I have seen M. Rison, and I see that it was a mistake. It was something the good farmer said that he would do if he were me. He does not understand the heart of a mother. Jean thought that I had said it. I came back to tell him, but he had taken his things and gone. Then I went to Babette. Madame knows of Babette?"

"His betrothed? O, yes."

"She loved him, Madame. It is dreadful to see her."

"Poor girl! I will go and try and comfort her," Madame said. That was her one idea when she heard of those in sorrow, to go to them, to see if there was anything that she could do to relieve or help them. ("'Pure religion and undefiled before God and the Father is this, to visit the widow and fatherless in their distress, and to keep oneself unspotted from the world.' I think always of Madame la Duchesse when I read that text in my breviary," M. le Curé said once to me long ago. "It just describes her.")

"It is very kind of Madame," the Mère Gilette said. "I am returning there myself. I did but come home to lock up the cottage for the night. I cannot leave her like that. It is not as if she had a mother or sister. Her father—he is good and kind, but a man is not like a woman at such times. He is furious with my poor Jean, and justly so, but it is no use to say that sort of thing to Babette; it only makes her worse. Madame understands?"

Madame de Mérillac bowed her head for answer. A few minutes later and they went out. It was very still. The people were away in the fields enjoying the evening breeze. Now and then they heard the clack of wooden *sabots*, or some old woman sitting on her door-step bade them good evening, but that was all. They went down the hill, passed close to the bridge and the shut forge, then turned to the left and went by the grey walls of the ruined castle till they came to the house of the farmer Rison. He was standing at the gate.

"She is just the same," he said to the Mère Gilette. Then he saw Madame, and bowed. "I do not think she quite understands at present that he is gone. She is like one who is light-headed —my poor little girl. If I had known she would take it thus I would have been less hasty." He drew back and opened the gate as he spoke, and Madame de Mérillac, followed by her late servant, passed up the path.

It was a pretty spacious farm-house that M. Rison inhabited. The door was open wide, and everything in the large old-fashioned kitchen looked clean and bright. Another time Madame would have remained to admire the rich carved wood-work, the quaint old-fashioned china, but now she scarcely noticed them, thinking only of the poor child they were going to comfort. She followed the Mère Gilette up the steep staircase, across a broad landing and into a pretty bedroom.

Babette was sitting just where the good Mère Gilette had left her, and in the same attitude. She turned her eyes for an instant on Madame de Mérillac, but directly afterwards she had resumed her old position, and was clasping and unclasping her hands, as one does in some grievous bodily pain. Madame knew Babette well by sight at church, but she had never before spoken to her. She was above the average height, with a pretty figure, already well developed, and possessed a very attractive pair of hazel eyes, while the brown hair, when the sun shone on it, was burnished here and there with gold. Generally the girl was very bright, and it was therefore a shock to Madame to see the change which a few hours had wrought. She was dressed in her best frock, a white muslin with pink ribbons here and there, while her straw hat trimmed with large daisies, lay on the ground near her. She had put on her best frock because a few days back Jean had promised to come and take her for a walk that evening, and she had been looking forward to it all day, and this was how it had ended. She could not believe in the evil which had befallen her. She had trusted Jean so, and he had said always that he loved her and wanted her to be his wife, and now—now he had gone away for ever.

"But he *said* he loved me," she said, looking up piteously at the Mère Gilette. "And he did once—O! I know he did—I know it. But he could not love me now, otherwise he would have stayed and worked and tried to change my father. Perhaps he has seen some other girl he likes better—some girl near B——, where he was always, always going lately," a piteous note of jealous pain sounding in the girl's voice.

"No, no, Babette, it is not that. It is a mistake, and it is me that he is angry with. He thought that I had been the means of bringing his conduct to your father's notice. That is why he is gone. I alone am to blame."

"But if he had loved me he would not have gone and left the place where I was," objected Babette.

"But, *ma chérie*, when young men get angry they forget everything else in their anger. In a little while it will wear off, and then Jean will return—I—I hope—I pray."

"But my father, he is full of wrath. He will not let Jean ever come to see me again, he says. O, why did he not stay, and work hard and get on? We might have been so happy—we might have been," and the great tears rolled down Babette's face.

"Cry, poor one," Madame said, speaking for

the first time, and taking Babette's hand in hers. "Tears will relieve you. It is when one cannot weep that it is worse," and she sighed. To weep had been always a difficulty with Madame de Mérillac. There had been days and nights after her Laure had been taken from her when she would have given all that she possessed for the relief of tears, and yet they would not come. It was only a long while afterwards that she had been able to weep. She sat beside Babette, holding her hands.

"It is better thus, far better," she said once or twice to Mère Gilette, and the peasant woman bowed her head. "When it is over she will sleep."

And by and by, when the sun had long set, and the stars were coming out one by one in the violet skies, Babette let herself be persuaded to undress and lie down in her neat little white bed, with the image of the dead Christ hanging above her head.

"I will come and see you to-morrow," Madame said softly, and Babette, poor gentle Babette looked up through her tears, and thanked her. Then Madame pressed her old servant's hand also. But to her she did not speak. What was it that she could say to console the heart of this mother? She could pray for her, that was all she could do. She went downstairs and out into the summer night. In the lane beyond the gate she met the farmer.

"She is better now," Madame said. "Tears have brought relief, and by and by nature will have its way and she will sleep."

"Madame is very kind. I thank her," M. Rison said. "It was my duty to put an end to it. I ought never to have consented. My girl should have done better, but as long as I thought well of him, it was enough for me that she cared for him and was happy; besides, in old days I, too, liked the lad. If he had chosen he might have done well, for there is some talent in the youth."

"He will return repentant and wiser, let us hope," Madame said, but M. Rison shook his head.

"He started for Paris, I hear. That is not the school in which to learn wisdom or penitence, I fear," the good farmer answered, shaking his head. Then Madame de Mérillac wished him good-night, and went on down the lane, and across the old stone bridge with the quiet river flowing beneath.

CHAPTER V.

"WE will find you work, never fear, never fear. Meanwhile make yourself easy, and enjoy a little of the pleasures of youth. For my part, I have passed all that. I care only now for a stoup of wine, a good dinner, and a little brandy after it —just to wash it down; but when one is young there are other things."

The speaker was a dirty-looking old man of about sixty, with watery eyes. He was dressed in a blouse, and on his head he wore a hairy cap, as he stood in the doorway of his house, which was situated in one of the lowest and most wretched parts of Paris. Jean, standing in front of him, thought him one of the most repulsive individuals he had ever seen. He was glad when a passer-by stopped to speak to his companion in a low voice, and gave him an excuse to retire. He nodded his head to the old man, and went away down the filthy smelling street, rendered more hideous by the harsh cries of the vendors of rotten fruit, and other such delicacies as come in the way of the dwellers of the Faubourg St. Antoine.

Jean had been in Paris only a few hours, and

already he was almost sick of the blinding glare and heat which belongs to the great capital in the dog-days. He was weary too, having travelled all through the summer night in one of those slow, stopping trains which generally follow the mail along the main lines of France, and which are hardly better than travelling by diligence. The morning was already well advanced when the train had crept into the great Terminus du Nord, and then Jean had had hard work to find an apartment suitable to his means; after which he had journeyed on foot to an address which had been given him by one of the lecturers who had spoken at the meeting on the green. "He would always find you a post," they had told Jean; and so the young man had gone down into the filthy low quarter in which the "Citizen Dobert," as he called himself, lived, who had promised to do even as the lecturer had said. Jean had cast aside, or professed to have cast aside, the religious principles in which he had been reared. He had taken to cursing and swearing, as did the men at the great mining works near B——; but he had nevertheless been startled and awe-struck by the filthy language and blasphemous oaths employed by the citizen. In the few minutes' interview he had had with him, the old man had crept close to him, and had told him of where he might go in order "to amuse himself." As he passed along the narrow, reeking streets, he was startled at the language of the low, dishevelled creatures, whose painted and powdered faces looked strange above their dirty finery. He was glad when he got away, out into the broader streets and so on till he came to the boulevards.

All day he wandered about the beautiful streets of the most beautiful city in the world, looking into the jewellers' windows in the Rue de Rivoli, or gazing up at the grand front of the Tuileries —grand in spite of the fact that the building was but a shell, and that the walls were black with the smoke of the fire. As he stood there, looking up, he could see through one of the windows the great candelabra still clinging to the wall—candelabra which once had been gilded, and full of lights, but were now blackened masses of metal. It was right and fitting, Jean told himself. That had once been the home of tyrants who had lived on the blood of the people. Still, as he looked at that wonderful ruin, it seemed a pity to have destroyed anything so grand and beautiful as the palace must once have been.

He grew weary of sight-seeing at last, and made his way to a small restaurant near where he had selected a lodging, and dined there off some unsavoury messes and a bottle of sour wine. The sun was gone, and the streets were cooler when Jean came forth from the close, hot eating-house. He sat down on a bench after a while, and smoked pipe after pipe, until long after the night had closed in, and the stars were shining in the great vault of heaven. He could see a few up above the roofs of the high, dirty houses. How beautiful they must look out in the country! Jean found himself sighing after his old place on the bridge, with the water lapping against the stone arches underneath, and for the sound of Gaspard's merry laugh, and the voices of his old companions. Ah, that belonged to the past, before he had heard of the rights and the freedom of man! He had done with that sort of thing, done with Gaspard and François, and the others who were content to labour all day long, and who went on Sundays and *fêtes* to hear the Mass of M. le Curé. He had done with it, he told himself again, and then rose up and made his way back to the quarter where the Citizen Dobert lived, back to a place of amusement where shameless women screamed filthy songs, and all was vile and low beyond description. Once, as he joined in the shouts of applause which greeted some indecency, the thought of Babette shot through the young man's brain—Babette, so good and innocent! The laughter died on his lips, and his face grew pale.

"What is it, my fine fellow, are you ill? Drink some of this," the woman beside him said, and she held up a glass of brandy.

He followed her advice. In a little while he had managed to banish the image of Babette from his mind, and was laughing again at the indecency and vileness around him.

The bells were sounding from the great churches for early Mass before Jean staggered along the street to his lodging, and flung himself on his wretched bed. It was past noon when he awoke. His eyes were heavy, and he felt as if his head would burst.

"It is the cursed brandy!" he told himself, as he stumbled down the narrow staircase to get his breakfast at the eating-house.

Now and again in those first days in that great city—that city famous for its marked contrasts, its lives of purest, noblest self-sacrifice, side by side with those devoted only to every vice that degrades—now and again, I say, thoughts of other days, when Babette was beside him, swept across Jean's memory, and he shivered in the sultry summer heat as though some unseen hand had smitten him. The hazel eyes seemed before him, and he read in them the condemnation of the life he led, and the depths to which he had sunk, but he put it all from him, fought against the recollection, and went away among his new friends, to vile men and yet viler women. A woman is always worse than a man if she is evil. I suppose it is because the God Who made them meant them, by their sweet and attractive purity, to lift us to better things. In that terrible time when the streets of the fair city of Paris were filled with blackened corpses, it was the women of the Commune who were the evil genius of that evil hour. They tell me—those who know, those who were there—that it was a sight that sickened the beholder, those mad, drunken furies, with their dishevelled hair and bare breasts, lying wounded in the streets, shrieking out curses until death came, and they could shriek no more.

Jean grew very weary of Paris before the dog-days ended. The heat, stifling and trying enough to a town-bred youth, was fearful to the young man reared in the sweet, fresh country air of Normandy. As he made his way along the wretched streets of the low quarter in which he habitually passed his time, he longed with a great longing for a sight of the green trees, the hills, and the silver river winding its way along under the shadows of the turrets of the *château* of Madame la Duchesse de Mérillac. Even if his pride would have allowed him to humble himself and return, he could not have gone, for he was no longer free. Old Dobert had found that Jean had a rough gift of eloquence, and almost nightly he was engaged in addressing meetings, telling the people of the wrongs they suffered, and how the hour was coming near when they must rise again and take back the power they wielded in 1793. If he would only have spoken more vehemently, old Dobert would have made him president of a section, but Jean could not cry out for blood.

"It is a mistake to kill," he said always, and Dobert laughed at him.

"You will mend of that," he said with a leer. "The taste for it comes with the power, my friend. It was sweet, the day we took the priests out and shot them. I liked it best when some were only wounded, and we had to prop them up to be fired at again. It would have made you laugh to hear them praying to God to have mercy, not upon themselves, but upon us! 'He is deaf, that God of yours—call louder,' I said to one old fellow—he was Curé of the church at the back here, and was badly wounded. He was leaning against the wall, but he opened his eyes then, and looked at me. 'Father, forgive him,' he said faintly; and then, 'He is not deaf, *mon ami*. He could hear that. Some day perhaps you will understand—I pray so, I pray so.' Then he fell down dead, and I kicked his body and came away."

Jean turned aside disgusted. Could it be after all that the others were right and he wrong? Could it be that there never yet lived a tyrant so terrible as King Mob? That was what M. le Curé, and Madame la Duchesse, and Turquin, and others in his Norman home had told him. "I kicked his body and came away." Could it be that after all, the people of the Commune were wrong? He could not—he would not—believe it. But still, the thought chilled him.

"What ails thee to-night? thou art lacking in thy usual eloquence," one of his friends said to him as they came away from the club-room. "It was of rosy lips that thou thoughtest rather than of tyrants and the rights of the people, I suspect. Well, well, it is good to be young. I forgive thee," and the other laughed and shook his companion's arm.

But Jean did not answer. Rosy lips! It was long since he had seen any, he thought bitterly. Who could apply such words to the painted, vile creatures with whom he consorted? and the face of Babette rose before him. He shuddered as the memory of his former betrothed smote on

F

him, just as some lost soul might shudder at the memory of those it had once known and loved, and from whom it was separated for ever more! Ah, those days! when he had wandered hand in hand with Babette in the woods around that far-off, goodly Norman village, and gathered sweet nosegays for her. He had given up that—given up all chance of being the husband of a maiden who had loved him well, given up the mother who had tended him and toiled for him as long as he could remember, given up Gaspard and François, and his fresh country life, given up everything for the cause of the people; at least so he told himself, and did not know that there was a good deal of pride and self-will mixed up with his determination. "For the people," he whispered to himself always. The Church had her martyrs. In the stained windows of the old Norman edifice where his little dead brother had served the Mass, there were pictures of those who had died because of the white Christ Who hung above the altar. Was he not a martyr as much as they? Had he not given up all because the people suffered? Surely his martyrdom was greater than those of the painted saints who had died believing that there was a God Who would reward them? The people were his God. As for the other—the Christ above the altar, before whom M. le Curé and Babette and his mother had knelt in prayer—He had been dethroned long ago. The people had disowned Him. "*A bas le Jésus,*" they had cried but yesterday, when a priest had come to a house in the Faubourg St. Antoine, where lay a poor fool in his death-agony, who had begged that the Curé of the parish might be sent for to hear his confession, and bring to him the Host, unreceived now for forty years. Yes, God was a myth. The people had decreed it so, and the people were always right, at least, so Jean believed then. So he went homeward to his wretched lodgings, and shivered as he thought of Babette whom he still loved. In the monotonous round of duty at the forge his love had perhaps cooled a little, but since he had left his home and was separated from her, truly all the old feeling had woke up. He tried to put the memory of her face from him, the face which came to him in his dreams, and looked at him so reproachfully.

The summer heats passed away at last, and winter came with its frost and snow. Jean's mind went back more than ever now to his Norman home. As he made his way to his lodging late from the club, where he had been busy with the Citizen Dobert, he thought of how the forest must look at home in its beautiful winter pall, and could see the wood-fire burning in his cottage home and throwing its gleams on the little Calvary in the corner.

The cold increased as the days went on. The very banks of the Seine were edged with ice. It was like the winter of 1870 to 1871—the winter which all who love France will never forget—when the sentries perished at their post outside the stone walls, and the hands of those who held muskets were frost-bitten while they sought ever to roll back the iron line which had swept round the once mighty capital.

"There will be skating soon if this lasts," Jean heard some one say, as he went to the house of the Citizen Dobert on the morning of Christmas Eve. Jean acted as a sort of secretary to the citizen, both in his private business as a wood-merchant, and also in his political character as a president of a revolutionary club. The wood business did not give Jean much trouble. All the subscriptions connected with the aims of the society were paid direct to the citizen, and perhaps if an audit of them had been called for, it would have been necessary to work harder at the wood business. As it was, there was no audit, and Dobert managed to live without any great trouble. His education had been neglected, and writing was a difficulty to him. A secretary was therefore almost a necessity, and Jean did not ask much, only just enough to enable him to live. He was serving the people, that was enough for him.

"It is cold, very cold," Citizen Dobert said, when his secretary made his appearance that morning of which I am writing. "In the parts from which you come the wolves must be hungry in the forest, eh?"

"Yes, there will be some hunting," the other answered, and his mind went back to the wide forest which he knew so well, just covered with winter's pall. Then he sighed and took up the letters which had come and set to work, only every now and then pictures of the home of his youth rose to his mind. It was late that night before he left the Citizen Dobert, past half-past eleven, and the frost was enough to freeze the very marrow in one's bones. As he walked homewards the church bells sounded for the midnight Mass. He shrugged his shoulders as he thought of the superstition of it all. It was nonsense, he knew that, but still, still he felt a vague longing to see the inside of the beautiful church at home again.

As he thought this, he found himself outside one of the noblest buildings in Paris. The bells had ceased, and he could hear the organ. He lifted the matting and passed in. The great lights on the altar were burning, and he could see the priests in their cloth of gold vestments, while the glorious plain chant one hears always in France, rose and fell under the lofty arches. And by and by came the *Gloria in excelsis Deo*, and after it the wonderful Gospel which tells of the shepherds who kept watch on the star-lit plains of Bethlehem eighteen hundred years and more ago. And even when it was over, Jean, though he was tired, could not make up his mind to go, but stayed on while the white clouds of incense rose, and the bell sounded, and the priest lifted up the Host before the people. And near where Jean stood was a young girl kneeling on a chair saying her rosary. Somehow she reminded him of Babette, though she was not really like her, only now and then when she glanced up at the high altar there was a look in her eyes which reminded him of the girl he had loved. He was sorry when the service was over and he had to return to his dirty lodging.

After Christmas the days seemed to creep more and more. Jean led a more quiet life now than he had done when first he came to Paris. Then he had delivered himself up to the company of the lowest among the low, had striven by wild excesses to put the memory of Babette from him, and for a time he had in a way succeeded. He had taught himself to believe that life with one woman would be stale and flat. After all, what had he in common, he asked himself, with this Norman girl, who went every day to pray in the church to the Christ Whom the people had abolished? But after a while he had grown sick of the painted creatures with their filthy witticisms, and had become grave and solemn, and devoted himself more than ever to the cause of the coming Social Revolution. His heart was sad for the people's misery and want. When he wandered along the great broad boulevards and saw the rich in their luxurious carriages, saw their houses resplendent with numerous lights and every magnificence that wealth could give, and noted their apparent indifference to the misery that existed scarcely a stone's-throw from them, he longed to drag them from their ease and make them taste of the chalice of the outcast. All one afternoon in the height of the Paris season he wandered through the fashionable streets, and in the evening spoke at a hall in the Faubourg St. Antoine. He had always had a sort of rough eloquence, but that night he spoke with passion and stirred his listeners.

"I would tear their jewels from them and trample them underfoot. I would fire their houses, these aristocrats who hate the poor. There is nothing like fire when you deal with vermin."

"Well spoken. You shall lead the way with a torch on the day we light fires in the streets of Paris again," the people answered, and they patted Jean on the shoulder, and would have *fêted* him, only he broke away from them. But even as he went, he heard the people calling out his own words, "Fire, that is the only thing to use in dealing with vermin."

"That was a fine speech you made the other night," the Citizen Dobert said to Jean a few days later. "The committee have ordered it to be printed and sent for distribution to all the chief towns where there are branches of the society."

Jean felt flattered: and when he saw himself in print he was proud. There was nothing in the speech, in reality, which could not have been demolished in five minutes by any man of education, but Jean did not know that. It was his first really violent speech, and its violence alone had led to its being printed.

"Cast your bread upon the waters, and you shall find it after many days." Jean read the speech through once or twice in print, and after a little, forgot it. It was only when many days and nights had come and gone that he remembered it, that his words came back to him!

CHAPTER VI.

THE winter rolled slowly away, and the springtime came at last. On the boulevards, vendors of flowers sold sweet-smelling violets and great bunches of white snowdrops, which the young children coming home from the Lenten services loved to stop and buy. It was pleasant out there in the wide streets in the sunlight, after the long, cold winter.

And by and by came Holy Week, with its veiled crucifixes and priests in sombre vestments, while at dusk the churches were thronged and the vaulted roofs overhead echoed to the mournful wail of the *Tenebræ* chant: *Miserere mei Deus, secundum magnam misericordiam tuam.*

It was superstition, Jean told himself, and yet somehow—perhaps for the sake of old memories, perhaps because he knew that at the same hour Babette would be in the parish church at home— the young man made his way on Good Friday to see Nôtre Dame in its black draperies, and hear the chanting of the Passion, and afterwards lingered on while the choir sang the plaintive reproach, *Popule meus, quid feci tibi, aut in quo contristavi te? Responde mihi*—lingered on till the Mass of the Presanctified was over and the altars were stripped, and Nôtre Dame was silent and deserted once more, save where here and there some worshipper knelt in silent prayer to the Christ Who, being lifted up according to His promise, draws all men who will unto Him.

But on Easter Day, when the church bells pealed, Jean did not go. He did not feel inclined for the joyous tones of the great feast. He stood outside, and watched the worshippers come forth with bright faces after the fulfilment of their sacred duties, but with it all he had neither part nor lot. He was as one of the crowd in the chanting of Good Friday's Passion, who answered the *Ecce Homo* of Pilate with the wild cry: *Non hunc, sed Barabbam.*

The summer came, and once more Jean thirsted for a sight of the green fields and winding silver streams of his Norman home. The heat of the Paris streets tried him, the noise of traffic by day and night grew horrible to him, but still he held on to his post. He would not desert the cause of the people. In the club-room, near the residence of the Citizen Dobert, he spoke often now, spoke with bitter hatred against those who lived in comfort.

"They exist but to devour you," he cried one sultry night, when overhead the thunder rolled as though telling of the storm to come, and the heat of the place was so intense that many of the women fainted, and were carried out. "They exist but to devour you, to amuse themselves, these aristocrats. I have seen them in their splendour, and I would burn their homes, and tear their ill-gotten gains from them!"

He spoke longer than he had ever done before. The enthusiasm of his audience pleased him. When he sat down, they raised cries for the erection of the guillotine. Then a whisper ran that there were *gendarmes* outside, and the cries ceased, and the company dispersed in silence. As Jean made his way through some of the side streets which led to his own lodging, it seemed to him that he was being followed. He looked back from time to time. An old man with white hair was behind him always. He stopped at last.

"Do you want anything?" he asked.

"I heard you speak," the other answered. "I, too, am interested in the sufferings of the people. That is my address. I have written it in pencil. Could you call on me there tomorrow? What hour would suit you?"

"I could call at four, not before," Jean answered.

"I will make it suit. Good-night." A moment later, and the old man was gone.

Jean looked at the address; there was no name, only No. 8, Rue de B——. The street was not more than a mile from where he lived. As he made his way homeward he wondered who and what the unknown was.

The next day Jean did his work with the Citizen Dobert, but left earlier than usual. The clocks of Paris were striking four as he rang the bell of No. 8 in the Rue de B——.

"I have an appointment here," he said to the old woman who opened the door. "Some monsieur invited me to call on him at this hour."

The old dame smiled, and invited him to enter. A minute later and he was in a large room on the ground floor, the walls of which were covered with well-filled book-cases. Near the empty hearth some one was standing in clerical dress. Jean looked, and, to his amazement, recognized the white-haired stranger of the previous evening. The old priest held out his hand, laughing good-naturedly.

"*Mon ami*," he said, "I have stolen a march on you, but you will forgive it because we are both interested in the same cause. No, I do not mean the Revolution—the picture yonder of my King will show you my politics—but I mean the cause of the poor, of the friends of Jesus Christ."

Jean did not answer for a moment, then he

said roughly: "Jesus Christ is dead. He does nothing. We have buried Him a hundred years back—in 1793."

"Are you *sure* of that?" the old priest asked. "If you will come with me a little, I will show you Him at work. I will show you some of His power, some of the wonderful things that He can do. Listen, my friend. I heard you speak. I go often to meetings, disguised as you saw me. My life is devoted to the cause of the poor, of the hungry, of the sinful. If you look in those cases you will see my name on the back of many covers. It may be that you have heard it. I am the Abbé Larmé."

Jean nodded. He knew the name. He had seen it often in large letters, posted up outside St. Roch and Nôtre Dame, and many other churches, as preaching for this charity or that.

"I heard you speak," the Abbé continued. "I listened, I marked your manner. I had heard you once before, and had noted that you spoke then with moderation—that where others cried out for blood and fire, you spoke only of how to obtain the wealth of the rich, and to distribute it to the poor. But last night you were changed, there was hatred in your tones; you, too, would cry out for blood. I listened, and then you told of your visit to the quarters of the wealthy, of your belief in their indifference, and so on. Well, if you will come with me, I will show you that they are not all like that: I will show you that the power of Jesus Christ is as great to-day as ever, that it has not grown weak, but that, on the contrary, it is still as capable as ever of leading men to the sublimest heights of self-sacrifice. Will you come?"

Jean hesitated.

"Why not?" the Abbé asked.

"If any one saw us together," Jean answered, "it might prejudice them against me. Those who think with me would fancy that I had deserted the cause."

"Then follow at a distance."

Jean nodded, and they set forth. The Abbé Larmé made his way in a contrary direction to that in which was situated the club-room and the residence of the Citizen Dobert, but still the quarter he went to was almost as low and vile. It was one of the poorest parts of Paris. By and by the priest stopped at the door of a wretched-looking habitation, and looking round made a sign to Jean to follow him in. At the top of the house they reached a back room. The staircase was rickety, and the rest of the house filthy enough, but here all was clean. The window was open, and a pot of flowers stood on the sill. Near the bed was a table, and on it a vase full of roses, a basin of jelly, and a crucifix. Lying on the couch was a young man of about five or six and twenty, and Jean saw at a glance that he was dying of decline. The invalid fixed his glassy eyes on Jean, as though inquiring who he might be.

"I have brought a friend with me, you see," the Abbé said, answering the look. "He is going round with me this afternoon to see some of my acquaintances who live in this neighbourhood. Tell me, *mon ami*, how have you passed the night?"

"Not well—the heat," the other answered faintly. It was so difficult to talk. The sands of life had run so low that there was hardly any breath left in that poor, wasted body.

"Has Madame visited you to-day?" the old priest asked.

The face of the dying man lighted up. "Not yet," he said. "The good Sister came as usual, and made me clean and the room tidy, but Madame said she should not be here till three or four o'clock. Listen! I hear someone coming. It is her footstep, I am sure."

Just then the door opened, and Jean saw a vision such as he had rarely seen before. It was a lady of some two or three and twenty, with masses of golden hair, and a face of extraordinary beauty. Never in all his life, he thought, had he seen anything surpassing the glorious grey eyes that looked so gently, so compassionately towards the sick-bed. She came slowly across the room, carrying in her hand a great bunch of creamy roses. Then her glance fell on the priest. As she gave him her hand she saw Jean, and lifted her eyebrows a little.

"I am late this afternoon," she said to the sick man, "but," smiling sweetly, "I went to all my other patients first, so that I might be able to stay longer with you." Then she took a chair and began to arrange the roses in an empty vase. Her voice was very sweet, Jean thought, like music. It brought back to his mind the tones of Mdlle. Laure, which in the old days at the *château* he had heard so often.

"Madame la Princesse is very good," the dying man returned. "There is nothing I like so much as these flowers. They remind me of long ago—of when I was little, and lived in the sweet, fresh country with my good mother—before I came to Paris—before I came——" shaking his head sadly.

Jean almost started. The words recalled his own case to him. Then the Princesse spoke, and he forgot all else listening to the silvery voice. Surely Mdlle. Laure had come back to earth, the tones were so similar. He could shut his eyes, and fancy he was back in the old *château*, in the long ago past.

"But I shall be vexed if my flowers make you look sad. I meant them to cheer you. Besides, no one is allowed to look sad to-day. It is the eve of a great feast—the feast of sinners. To-morrow is the day when the Church commemorates the Assumption of the Mother of God—that Mother whose children we became amidst the darkness of the first Good Friday, and whose arms are ever stretched out to the sad and the sinful. But see," laughing a little gently, "I am usurping the functions of M. l'Abbé there. If I am quiet, perhaps he will tell us some wonderful things."

The priest shook his head and rose. "I delegate my task to Madame la Princesse," he said. "I am taking my young friend round with me to-day. *Mon ami*," touching the hand of the sick man, "I will see M. le Curé, and arrange with him that to-morrow at seven o'clock he shall bring you our Divine Lord in the Holy Communion. As Madame says, 'It is the feast of us sinners.' It is well not to miss it."

Then the Abbé blessed the occupant of the couch, and bowed to the lady, and Jean followed him from the room. As they passed out into the narrow, hot street, reeking of filthy odours, he wondered how one so fair and beautiful as the vision he had just seen could come to such a place.

"She is very lovely," he said, half to himself. "What is her name?"

"She is the Princesse Calachieri. Her husband is a Neapolitan, but the Princesse is by birth a Sicilian. The beauty of a Sicilian blonde is proverbial, but beauty of the body is but a poor thing, *mon ami*. It goes quickly, and at best, what remains of it after death? Madame la Princesse has that which is better—she has the beauty of a soul devoted to the cause of Jesus Christ and His poor."

So there were others besides the Communists who thought of the poor, Jean reflected. Here were a priest and an aristocrat both trying to help them. Then they entered another house, and his train of thought was broken in upon.

In a small, dark room at the back of the dwelling, they found a little old man, quite blind, and engaged in dusting his room was a very stout lady, one of the stoutest ladies, Jean thought, he had ever seen in his life. When she saw the Abbé she began to laugh.

"It is nearly done," she said. "Some of my

friends of the Association say to me it is the talking they find so difficult, and I say always, 'O my dears, that is nothing to me, it is the sweeping and the dusting that try me,' but then they are not forty-six inches round the waist, as I am, so I suppose that makes a difference."

"No doubt, no doubt," the Abbé responded, laughing. "And our poor friend here, how is it with him to-day?"

The lady shook her head, and across her countenance there came a look of compassion. Naturally she was very plain, but when that look came, she seemed to Jean almost beautiful.

"It is not a very good day," she said gently. "We feel the full weight of our cross just now."

So the Abbé Larmé sat down beside the blind old man and began to talk; but it was difficult to get much out of him. He complained of the dust which Madame made by sweeping. It had upon him the effect of snuff. For his part, he would prefer to be without this sweeping. The Abbé sympathized with him in his discomfort, but ventured to suggest that Madame's soups and jellies and tobacco perhaps made up for it, and that therefore one must put up with her little whim about cleanliness. But it was no good. As Madame had said, 'It was a bad day,' and the Abbé went away after a while, having the tact to see that that afternoon at all events it would not do to touch on serious topics.

"Who was the lady?" Jean asked, when again they were in the street.

"It is Madame Plantier, the wife of a great merchant, who loves to devote some of her wealth and leisure to the relief of the sufferings of others," was the reply.

Jean followed his companion still thoughtfully.

So through the long, hot hours in the filthy, crowded streets of one of the poorest parts of Paris, they went from house to house, now to a garret at some dizzy height, now into some cellar where scarce a ray of light or a breath of air penetrated, and everywhere they found members of the Association, which the Abbé had founded, at their work. As they left each place, Jean asked the names of the visitors. Some among them were those of the noblest houses of France, while others were the wives and daughters of ordinary citizens. And at one place, almost the last they visited, they found a simple, kindly lady dressed in black, but instead of sitting down, the Abbé stood before her, so Jean, not knowing why, stood also. The lady's work was just finished, so the priest said he would go with her through the streets to her carriage, and Jean followed. At a little distance they found a small, plain brougham, with nothing very smart about it, not like the grand carriages which Jean had sometimes contemplated in the Bois, and the only thing about it which struck him as odd was the fact that whilst the lady was getting into the vehicle, the coachman sat with his hat off, while the footman and the Abbé, who stood at the door, had theirs in their hands also. Then the little carriage rolled away, and Jean learned to his amazement that the simple kindly lady was a king's grand-daughter, and one of the house which for seven hundred years had reigned over France. He began to think he had made a mistake in some things. These great persons were not all bad. Still, why should they be superior to any one else? All men should be equal. Then the Abbé spoke to him, and his train of thought was interrupted.

"*Mon ami*," he said, "I thank you for your complaisance in coming with me to-day. I could wish that the leaders of your party would show the same liberality, but they will see nothing but what they wish to see, believe nothing but what they wish to believe. But now that you have come, and have seen, you will not make those sweeping assertions that no one among the upper classes cares for the sufferings of the poor. You have seen my Association. It consists only of the class of those you attack, I mean the wealthy, or, at all events, those who do not work for their living. Most of the ladies you have seen to-day have beautiful homes in the country, to which they could go in this hot weather, and yet no! here they stay, helping the poor. They arrange for their holidays just as if they were shop-folk—turn and turn about. If, however, family duties, a husband's pleasure, a parent's wishes, anything of that sort, makes it prudent to go, then they simply intimate the fact to me, and I see that some one else fulfils their work till they can return. It may be two or three years, perhaps, before they come back, but it makes no difference. They are still members of the Association. The only thing required of them is, that wherever they are, should occasion arise, they will assist as much as lies in their power the poor, the sad, and the sinful. Come, *mon ami*, is not the Association of the Compassionate Heart of the Good Shepherd a fine one?"

Jean nodded. He could not deny it, and yet it had to do with religion, and the Commune was at war with religion. He did not know what to say.

"Then I have proved my case," the priest

said. "'Come and see—the upper classes are not all indifferent,' I said to you, 'and Jesus Christ is not dead, but working still.' You have seen His power. It cannot be pleasant—it is evident that it is against what is natural—to see delicately-nurtured ladies working at such duties as you have seen them to-day. It is the love of Jesus Christ, the love of His poor, which is leading them to conquer themselves, to go where it is hot, and stifling, and dirty, and inodorous. No, my friend, Christianity is not dead, any more than you are. It is more alive than it was ages ago. Then, men committed crimes, and thought to atone for them by adding a new chapel to this church, or a new aisle to that. But our Christianity of to-day, where it exists, is of a higher order. Men who practise it seek to conquer *self*, and refrain from the crimes which stained the so-called ages of faith. *Mon ami, mon ami!* disbelieve your leaders when they tell you that the religion in which you were born is dead. In their health and their strength they say it, but when death comes—O what a change! We priests see this. It is an every-day occurrence. *A bas le Jésus!* they say when they are well, but when sickness comes, they send for the Curé— they want to get back to the Jesus they despised. But the hour is late, and I have to preach at eight o'clock in the chapel of the good Nuns of the Visitation. My friend, I wish you goodnight, and I pray God to bless you—you and those dear to you," and the old man smiled a gentle kindly smile.

Jean took the outstretched hand. He had felt irritated when the Abbé had spoken of the cowardice of atheists in their death-hour, but his angry feelings melted away at the blessing "Those dear to you." It seemed to Jean that he had blessed Babette—Babette, and his mother, and Gaspard, and François, and many others in that far-off home of his, to which, like all the sons of Normandy, his heart ever turned. He shook the priest's hand warmly, and turned away and went home. And that evening he did not go to his usual haunts, but sat alone, thinking.

"They are not all bad, these nobles," he said the next time he spoke in the club-room, but the people would not hear him, and shouted him down. They liked it when he had called out for blood, but to praise these aristocrats, that was not to be borne. In the morning, the Citizen Dobert reproved him. He said to speak like that was to sin against the people. Jean must never do it again. It was all very well for the Moderates in the Chamber, but as the assistant of a member of the Commune——!

Jean said nothing. What was the use? Besides, what did it matter if a few of these aristocrats were misjudged? As a race they were vile, and, no doubt, should be exterminated.

August passed, and September. People began to return from the sea-side, and a few even from their *châteaux*, to the fashionable quarter of Paris. Jean rarely went there now. He had seen all the sights long ago. He had meant to go and pay a visit to the old Abbé Larmé again, as he had promised, but he put it off until at length he decided that the time for going had gone by. He forgot the other side to the great question, and was only reminded of it all accidentally one gusty October morning when passing across the Place in front of Nôtre Dame. There was a crowd filing into the Cathedral, and he stopped to ask a woman what it meant.

"It is the funeral of Monsieur l'Abbé Larmé, the founder of the Association of the Compassionate Heart of the Good Shepherd. Monsieur must have heard of it? The funeral Mass is about to begin. The Archbishop of Paris himself will, it is said, preach the sermon."

Jean was sorry. The memory of the kind, eager old man came back to him, and he was vexed that he had not visited him again as he had promised. It was too late now, like so many things we put off doing. The only thing Jean could do was to pay a last tribute of respect. He followed the crowd into the great, dim edifice. Along the nave from pillar to pillar were stretched black hangings, with the Abbé's initials in silver letters embroidered on them, while in the centre, on a catafalque surrounded by hundreds of tapers, was the coffin. The great candles on the high altar were lighted, the priests in black vestments were in the sanctuary, the Archbishop of Paris was on his throne, surrounded by the Chapter, and under the grey arches the plain chant *Kyrie* rose and fell. And by and by there was a hush as the successor of the martyred Archbishop Darboy ascended the pulpit and, holding his crozier in his hand, gave forth his text: *Euge serve bone et fidelis, intra in gaudium Domini tui*— "Well done, good and faithful servant, enter into the joy of thy Lord."

And then the Archbishop told of the great life which had passed away, of how from boyhood it had been lived for Jesus Christ, how self had had neither part nor lot in it, how all ranks of society were alike dear to him, and how that day proved it, as gathered round that catafalque were men and women from the very highest to the very lowest.

"He has gone from amongst us," the Archbishop cried with outstretched arms, "but he has provided for the carrying on of his work. He has passed away, but his memory we shall hold in fond remembrance. 'In the sight of the unwise he has seemed to die,' but his soul is with God, and he has gone, as we believe, and hope, and pray, to receive the just reward of his life, gone to where the souls of the righteous are made perfect, gone to enter into the joy of his Lord."

And then the Archbishop made his way back to his throne, and the Mass was continued. And by and by the Host was lifted up between heaven and earth for the soul of the departed, and no sound broke the hush of the great Cathedral save the clink of the swinging censers. And then the west doors rolled back, and overhead the great bells began to peal, slowly, softly, sadly, it is true, but yet they pealed, while the shuffling tramp of the bearers mingled with the chanting of the choir: *In paradisum deducant te Angeli. Chorus Angelorum te suscipiat, et cum Lazaro quondam paupere æternam habeas requiem.*

It was a dream, a superstition, for which this man had lived, Jean told himself as he wandered along the streets once more, and yet—yet how beautiful! The words of the Archbishop rang in his ear. The look of confidence upon his face was before his eyes. Was it all a dream? His mother did not think so, nor Babette—his Babette, no! not his, some other happy man's Babette. He had flung away that chance. Had he not been a fool to act as he had done to adopt views which parted him from such a girl? He had grown tired of the regular work of the sweet, quiet, homely village, grown tired of his duties, and had come forth to serve the people. Were the people much better off because he had lived in filthy lodgings amongst wretched beings, and acted as secretary to such a one as the Citizen Dobert? Perhaps after all it would have been better if he had stayed at home and minded M. le Curé always. He would not have been parted then from Babette. And as the days went on this train of thought came often to Jean's mind, and with it a great longing to see again the face of his former betrothed.

Winter set in early that year, and in France there was much distress. Every department of trade seemed depressed, and yet the *employés* were continually demanding more wages. The journals were full of it. For the thoughtful it was a time of uneasiness. The Citizen Dobert and those who shared his opinions rubbed their hands.

"It is coming; all this helps our game. It is the first movement of the Social Revolution, of the time when we shall make them disgorge their wealth, these tyrants who ought to sneeze in the sack, as they used to say in the good days of 1793."

Jean did not answer; he scarcely heard. He was weary of it all, and he wanted to see Babette, wanted to see his old home and his mother's face once more. Would he ever do so, he wondered. He was still too proud to go back and humble himself, and he had enough faith left in his cause to enable him to remain true to it.

The month of December came, and with it a hard frost and a biting east wind.

"You know B——?" the Citizen Dobert asked one morning. The town in question was an old cathedral city not above twenty miles from Jean's home. He answered that he knew each stone of it.

"Good. There is trouble at the mines near. The men want stirring up. The committee have decided to entrust the task to you. I forget the name of the owner, but it is no matter."

Jean told him. It was Blondel. He had a *château* not a mile beyond the village where Jean had been brought up.

"That is it," Dobert answered. "When can you start?"

"To-morrow," he replied promptly. His heart beat quickly. He was getting weary of the cause, but B—— was near his old home. Perhaps he might see Babette: perhaps—who could tell?

The next day he left Paris. Would he ever see it again, he wondered vaguely, as its spires and domes faded from sight. If he did not, he did not care. He sat motionless, gazing out of the window at the flying landscape. It was nearly two years since he had seen the country, and though the trees were bare and the ponds frozen, to Jean it had never seemed so beautiful.

And when the day had faded away and the wintry twilight was falling fast, he saw the glorious Cathedral towering up above the roofs of the houses of B——, and knew that scarce twenty miles off were his home, his mother, and Babette.

CHAPTER VII.

THE snow was falling quite fast. The roofs of the quaint old village near which Babette lived were white already, though the snow had not been coming down more than a quarter of an hour. "If it went on like this for any length of time, they would be snowed up as they were last winter," M. Rison said, as he came into the large, old-fashioned kitchen, and stood on the mat shaking the flakes off his boots. "Did Babette remember?" he asked.

Babette with her hazel eyes and golden brown hair, was standing in one of the windows looking out. She was dressed in a black serge, with a white apron, while in her ears were a pair of long silver ear-rings, and she looked very nice —very nice, but with a sad little look about her —a look which was always there now. Yes, Babette had known what it was to be very wretched, known what it was to wish in the morning that it was evening, and in the evening that it was morning. For many weeks after Jean's departure she had lain on her bed, too weak almost to speak, and the summer had gone, and the trees round her home were crimson and gold with autumn's tints before she had been able to come downstairs and set about her daily tasks again. "Did Babette remember," M. Rison asked, "that snow-storm?"

Babette nodded. Somehow the thought of anything which was past seemed to recall Jean to her. Those had been the early days of her sorrow; at least, he had only left her some six months then. She remembered how she had wondered where he was, and if he was cold, and dreaded that perhaps he was without shelter. Once he had loved her, even as she herself loved him, Babette thought, as she stood watching the white flakes fall, on the day of which I write. Why had he ever gone away with those wicked men who denied God, and who wanted to rob her father of his honest earnings, and take his fortune for themselves, or give it to others who had no money because they were too lazy to work for it. Ah, if those horrid lecturers had never come that day to the green, perhaps Jean would have been content to remain at home, and when he had got a little more money, then he would have married her. But no, she remembered that even before that, a certain restlessness—an impatience of his work—had come on him. That sweet dream was over now. Jean had gone a great way off, some said to Paris, others to Lyons, none knew for certain, and he would never come back, so she would never be wedded. Her father talked to her of this young man and that, and brought them to the house because they had sued hard to be introduced to her, but she was indifferent to them all. She was a faithful girl, and had given her heart right loyally to her former lover, and something told her she would never care for any one like that again.

Then Babette roused herself suddenly from the train of thought into which she had fallen, and, taking off her muslin apron, put on her hat, and began to wrap herself up in a thick, warm cloak.

"It is cold for my girl to go out," the farmer said. "Is it not better, Babette, to stay in the warm chimney corner this wintry afternoon?"

But the girl shook her head. "I am going to the church, and then to the *château*. I have done some work that Madame la Duchesse wanted much, some shawls for her poor. She is going to give them to some of the old women after Mass to-morrow. It will help to keep their poor shoulders warm. Yes, that is what the big parcel contains." Then Babette, having kissed her father, set out.

M. Rison's house was situated just outside the village, and Babette made her way along a narrow lane till she came to the walls of an old ruined castle. Then she turned to the right, through a couple of archways, crossed the principal street of the hamlet, and made her way into the beautiful old church.

Babette did not have to wait long for her turn. There were not many people present that cold Saturday afternoon, and it did not take her two minutes to make her confession to M. le Curé. Then she went round to the chapel of the Blessed Sacrament and gave thanks that her soul was now white and clean once more—not that it had ever been very black, for a more devoted Christian than M. Rison's daughter never lived.

And then she left the great church which she loved so well, and hurried along the road, past the ivy-covered walls, and through the coronet-crowned gates up to the *château*, with its many turrets and pointed towers. It was almost dark when she got there, and the snow was coming down faster than ever.

Babette followed the servant across the hall and along the corridor, through the great deserted drawing-room into the little sitting-room, which the lady of the mansion always inhabited now.

"Madame la Duchesse had been out in the snow and had got wet. She would be down shortly," the old servant said, and went away leaving the girl alone in the pretty chamber, which was situated on the ground floor of one of the towers.

A wood fire was blazing on the hearth, and that, with a carefully shaded reading lamp, was all the light the turret-chamber had. It was a lofty little apartment, and the walls were panelled with old embroidered silk, and there were consequently no pictures, only on both sides of the fire-place were hung cases filled with miniatures. The furniture, like that of the great drawing-room, was in the style of Louis Quatorze, and there were numerous little tables on which were photographs of members of the House of France, and other distinguished persons. But on the table situated close to the arm-chair in which Madame always sat, was only one picture, namely, that of her dead daughter. Babette was never tired of looking at that picture. She could remember quite well when she was a child, envying Mdlle. Laure her beauty and her pretty frocks. She went now and stood in front of it. Yes, it was very like. She could even remember the dress—it was a soft grey one, with silver buttons on it. And there were the beautiful eyes, and the soft brown hair, looking just as they used to look in life. Then the door of the turret-chamber opened, and Madame la Duchesse, in her long trailing black draperies, entered. She smiled when she saw what Babette was about.

"*Mon enfant*," she said, "I fear I have kept thee waiting, but I have been round to see several of my poor neighbours, and then, even though it was snowing, I wanted to pay a visit to the cemetery. I do not like to miss that if I can help it, so I went. But my dress got damp, and I had already begun to put on my evening robe before thy name was brought to me. Sit down, Babette, and warm thyself this cold night. I fear thy cloak is wet."

Babette gave a little laugh. It was rarely that she did so now, but it struck her as curious for her to think of wet things, she who never stayed in, whatever the weather was.

"Madame must forgive me," she said in her gentle way, "but I am accustomed to get wet. I remember the time when I loved to tumble in the snow, but that was long ago now."

"So I suppose, Babette," Madame de Mérillac answered. "At your age one ceases to do those things. It would not look well," and the lady almost laughed herself.

"But all the same I would like to have done it this afternoon, when I saw the ground getting whiter and whiter," and Babette gave a nod with her head, so that this time Madame laughed outright. Then the sound seemed to startle her. Laughter was a thing not often heard in the sombre *château* now. Once it had been the order of the day, when Monsieur le Duc had been alive, and Laure in her pretty frocks had skipped along the galleries; but since the day the second procession had wound its way along the avenue, under the green branches, and the *Requiem æternam* of the priests had hushed the song of the birds, it had become a thing of the past.

"This child makes me forget my sorrows for a while," Madame said, placing her slender, jewelled hand on Babette's shoulder, "and yet she is a strange person to do so, for she has known what it is to have a heartache."

Babette's hazel eyes filled with tears, and across her face stole a look of pain. "If I could only see him again," she whispered. "If I could only see him, because I love him. Perhaps I ought not to say so, but I cannot help it."

"And you have never heard of him, young one, since the day he went away?"

Babette shook her head. "My father forbade his ever writing or speaking to me again. It is better not to speak of it," she said, "if Madame will forgive me for saying so. I cannot do it. By and bye, perhaps I shall be able to do so, but that time is not yet."

Madame de Mérillac softly patted the girl's shoulder, and turned the conversation to the parcel which Babette had brought with her.

"They are exactly what I require. She has neat hands, this child," Madame said, as she put one of the little grey shawls over her shoulders to see the effect. They were of the kind which in England are called 'Hug-me-tights.' "These will do, Babette. After Mass to-morrow I shall go round with them. I think that you must come also. The pleasure of the poor souls will reward you for the trouble. Now, see, that is the money for the wools, and that the price of the shawls. There ought to be something for all the time too, I think. Look round, child, and tell me if there is anything in the room which has taken your fancy, this work-box perhaps, or that little silver basket. Come, tell me what you would like?"

Babette was silent for a moment, and then she looked up shyly at her hostess. "If it is not asking too much," she whispered, "I should like a picture of Mdlle. Laure."

"You will value it if I give it?" Madame de Mérillac asked gravely.

"Indeed, indeed, yes, Madame," Babette answered earnestly.

The Duchess walked across to a cabinet which

stood near the door, and unlocking a drawer, drew forth several photographs.

"This is the one from which the large painting there on China was done. Would you like it, or do you prefer some other?"

"I should like this, if Madame can spare it," choosing one of those in which the girl was depicted in a grey dress with silver buttons. "I remember her so well like that."

Madame de Mérillac bent her head. Then she looked round the room. She wanted a frame for her dead child's picture. Those near her did not seem good enough. Then her eyes fell on one made of mother-of-pearl, and taking the photograph out of it, she slipped into its place Laure's sweet face.

"I could not give you anything I value more," she said, as she gave the present to her guest.

Babette tried to thank her, and failed. The face of Madame, so sad, and yet so resigned, touched her deeply. The hazel eyes filled with tears. Madame de Mérillac pressed the girl's hand.

"Take care of yourself, child," she said, as she wished her good-night. "And to-morrow, after *Grande Messe*, you will wait for me at the west door, and we will take round your beautifully worked shawls. Does it still snow, Gaspard?" she asked of the old butler.

"But yes, certainly, Madame," was the reply. "There has not, it is said, been such a night for many years."

"Then let Jacques see her down the avenue. If he take a lantern there will be less fear of their falling into the stream," the Duchess ordered, and then, after wishing Babette once more good-night, went back to her solitary turret-chamber, and sat listening to the wind which moaned and whistled round the house, while the logs smouldered on the hearth, and she told chaplet after chaplet on her rosary for the souls she had loved and lost.

"Good-night—no, indeed, I can get along all right," Babette said to the servant, who had lighted her down the avenue, and proposed seeing her to the end of the road which came out on to the bridge under which the river flowed. "It is not far. I shall do very well."

The girl, with her cloak wrapped tightly round her, walked rapidly on, but it was hard work. Every moment the snow was getting deeper and deeper, the flakes were coming down so thickly, that it was difficult to see a few steps even in advance, while the wind from the northeast felt like a razor to the face. Babette bent down her head to avoid the blast, and she soon felt rather sorry that she had not allowed Jacques to see her as far as the bridge. In the distance she could hear the sound of the Angelus pealing from the great tower of the church, and the silvery notes gave her confidence. She made the sign of the cross on her breast, and went forward more bravely. The Blessed Mother and the holy angels could see her and take care of her just as well in the midst of the darkness and the blinding snow as in the broad light of day. Nothing could happen to her unless it was God's will. M. le Curé had often told her that, and she knew he was right. After all, what would it matter if she was lost in the snow? She would only feel very tired and lie down and sleep, and never wake up again any more in this world. Surely there was nothing much to dread in that? Almost every morning when she awoke and the thought of her lost lover came back to her, she felt a longing to sleep again for evermore. It would only be a sort of fulfilling of her wish. And then, M. le Curé had so often told her death was nothing, that it was quickly over, and that it was but the entrance into eternal life.

But stay, would she really like to die? Babette stood still to ask herself this question. No, after all, in spite of what she had thought, she knew she did not wish it, because, deep down in her heart, so deep that neither her father nor the Mère

Gilette nor M. le Curé himself suspected it, there was just one faint ray of hope left that even yet, after all this weary time, her Jean would come back to her. In the old days of their courtship he had loved her: Babette was sure of that. Perhaps some day the thought of her would visit him, the remembrance of those happy bygone times come back to him, and he would rise up and return, and plead first for her father's forgiveness and then for hers. She would not give it him just at once, not the very moment he asked, because he deserved to be punished, and in the old days she had liked now and again to tease him. O how happy she would be if he came back, having renounced his opinions and pleaded to her father! She could never care for any one after Jean. Perhaps, perhaps even yet it might be! She would ask the Holy Mother to obtain for her this favour. The dear Lord would never refuse what Mary asked.

And so the young girl, in the midst of the darkness and the storm, with a heart full of faith, looked up towards the heavens, and asked that, before very long, her Jean might be brought back to her, and that the Mère Gilette might be comforted once more.

"She has known so many sorrows, this poor one," she whispered. "She is alone, her husband

and her children have been taken from her by death, all save this one. Restore him to her, thou who hast known anguish greater than any other mother. Rescue him from evil companions. Be to him and to me a Mother of Compassion."

Babette ceased. It was a long way off to Heaven, but M. le Curé said that made no difference. Would the Holy Mother answer her prayer, she wondered; and then, drawing her cloak tighter, she once more set forth on her journey, and as she did so she heard far away in the distance the low rumble of the *diligence* from B——.

It was quite half-past six when Babette crossed the bridge, and just then the heavy *diligence*, with its lamps looking like fiery eyes, rolled by her, and a moment later rattled under the arch into the little courtyard of the hotel. She knew the driver, old Vojon, and had half a mind to stop and ask him how he was. It must have been a bad journey, but it would be nothing to the return one. The *diligence*, which carried the mails, was timed to set out at midnight, and it would be five in the morning before it got back to B——. Poor Vojon!

And yet, cold and disagreeable as the weather was, Babette, when she reached the old castle, did not turn to the right to go home, but went instead up the steep little Grande Rue to the house of the Mère Gilette.

The widow was sitting by a bright wood fire knitting, when Babette, having tapped, was called on to come in. There was no light but that which came from the ruddy blaze on the hearth, and the red gleams played cheerfully on the white-washed walls, and on the little Calvary in the corner, where stood the dusty wisps of corn which the brown hands of little Claude-Marie had fixed there so long ago, on the eve of the feast of the great Mother of God.

Across the face of the Mère Gilette there shot a look of pleasure when she saw who her visitor was. She rose, but not so quickly as she had been wont to do, for her many trials had begun to tell. She had been through the furnace of great suffering. All her life had been passed in that quiet Norman hamlet. She had lived with her parents, until they died, in the old farmhouse down by the river, and then had come the time at the *château* when she had been in the service of Madame la Duchesse, whom she would never have left, but for the good Gilette.

After that had come a period of mingled sorrows and joys, as one by one the children that were born to her were taken from her to rest in the cemetery on the hill. And then had come the day when the partner of her life had been carried in through those wooden gates, and been placed beside his dead children. That had been a day the Mère Gilette would never forget.

At last it had come that she had but one treasure left her—her Jean. And it was not until he had gone from her—gone, not like the rest, up the hill, with the blessing of the Church, but away with evil companions to Paris—the Paris which had shot down like dogs the men of God in the May of 1871—that she sank down under the weight of her cross. She had borne up bravely through those other trials. The consolations of the Church had been hers. God had but taken those she loved to be with Him in Paradise, but what comfort could she have in this last terrible blow? Till that had come she had seemed young. Now her hair was grey, her body was bent, and when she moved, she did so feebly. Often of late Babette had noticed this, but, on the winter's night of which I write it struck her more forcibly than ever. Mère Gilette folded the girl tenderly in her arms, and then sank back into her seat.

"It is a stormy night for you to be out, my child," she said. "The good father will be anxious, I fear."

"He thinks I am at the *château*," Babette answered. "I went to take Madame some shawls she had given me an order to work for her, and I stayed a long time, and—O look what she has given me as a reward for my work!" and the girl held out the picture in its exquisite frame.

The Mère Gilette took it gently, reverently, into her hands. She had guessed whose picture it was. The tears came into the elder woman's eyes as she looked down at the sweet face she had known so well. She had been at the *château* the day Mdlle. Laure had been born, and she had been there the day she had died, for when the period of sickness and rapid decline set in, the Mère Gilette had gone back to help in nursing the Duchess's daughter. She looked at the picture long, shaking her head sadly, then she handed it back to Babette, and wiped away the tears.

"One should not sorrow for one so sweet and good as she was," she said softly. "When the flowers of earth are ripe for Heaven, they are gathered, that is all. Why should one grieve, I say, because the Lord of the harvest sent for her in all her purity and innocence? It is well with her soul, I doubt it not."

The Mère Gilette ceased to speak, and sat gazing at the burning embers. Outside the wind moaned, and nothing broke the stillness save the sudden movement of one of the outside shutters, as though some one had pressed it. She looked round quickly then.

"It was but the wind," Babette said.

The Mère Gillete rose. Across her face had stolen a curious look, a look of hope. She moved to the door, and opening it, peered out into the night. The snow was falling fast. There was nothing to be seen. 'Twas but the wind. The light on the woman's face faded away. She came back, and resumed her old attitude, only every now and then she seemed to listen, listen! She forgot the girl, forgot everything then in one great longing to look once more upon the face of her boy.

"Let it be, let it be," she prayed always. "If I may see his face, and know that he is safe at home, then I shall be content to go, glad to go."

And so she prayed now; and outside the wind howled, and the snow fell, but the shutter, the shutter was still. It did not move again. The light upon the face had gone out. The time went on. The warmth of the fire was pleasant, Babette thought. She ought to go home, but she did not want to do so. She liked being where she was, being with Jean's mother. Now and then she glanced up at her companion's countenance, and every time she did so, a pang shot through her heart. There was such agony upon the face. Surely Mary must have looked something like that the day she had stood by the Cross, while through the encircling gloom the cry of the Man-God rang forth, *Eli, Eli, lama sabacthani!*

By and by Babette softly touched Mère Gilette's hand. "It is time to go," she said.

"My pretty one," the elder woman answered. "And I have been sitting here, thinking sad thoughts, when instead I should have been chatting with you." She was vexed with herself. Her Jean's choice! and to treat her like that! "My pretty one," she said again.

"I did not care about the talking," Babette answered in her soft, pleasant voice. "We were thinking of the same thing, and I am quite content to be silent." Once it had been different with the girl, but that was two years ago now. "And then I like to be here with you, his mother," she added.

"You love him still, my Babette?" Mère Gilette said.

The girl nodded.

"May *le bon Dieu* shower His blessings on you, pretty one. It is good of you; it comforts me. Look you, there are many who say to me that he has gone among evil companions, that he works for an evil cause, the cause of those who deny the good God, and keep the House of France in exile, and they seem to think that I should be angry with him, and glad that he comes not to my door. They do not understand. The heart of a mother is not thus. He is my son. It is enough. Though all the world should turn their backs upon him, yet will not I. Love him still, my Babette. He is not all bad. He was weary with his rough work, which was distasteful to him, and the restlessness of youth was on him, and then came those who tempted him away. But if he returns some day to see the face of his old mother once more before she dies, and finds that his Babette is true to him in spite of all, then he will be won back to better ways, and perchance your father will forgive him and let it be. An evil woman will drag with ease the soul of a man down to Hell, but on the other hand, to what a height may not a good one raise him? Be to him as an angel guardian, Babette, if he should return, and I—I am not here. Sometimes it seems to me as if the day was not far distant, as if my little Claude-Marie and those other dear ones called for me. May be it is but an old woman's fancy, but it seems so, it seems so."

"Do not talk so," Babette answered. "It pains

me. I want you, and Jean will want you, I *know* he will. He is only led away for a time. He will return, and we shall be happy once more. You must wait and share with us those good days, you must."

But the Mère Gilette did not answer. She only smiled and shook her head. "*Le bon Dieu* have thee in His keeping," she said, and kissed the girl good-night.

The storm was as bad as ever, Babette found, as she stepped forth from the little cottage, and O how deep the snow was! If it had not been coming down so thickly, it would have been easy enough to see, for when the white snow is lying it will make light the blackest night, just as in the darkness of sorrow the sufferings of the Man-God shine forth to console and sustain the heart of the mourner.

Babette went down the steep hill of the little Grande Rue without meeting a single person. More than once, though the snow was almost ankle-deep, she thought she heard the sound of some one behind her, but every time she paused there was nothing to be seen, and though she waited, no one came in sight. She went on again at last impatiently. The wet snow was getting through her boots, and *mon Dieu!* how the wind cut through one, she thought, as she fought against it across the deserted courtyard of the old ruined castle, and along the lane to her home. She had meant to rise for early Mass to-morrow, but she was afraid that if the storm continued they would have to wait to go to church till they were dug out. She would be sorry if she could not receive Holy Communion. She had meant to offer it for Jean. Well, she must be content to offer her Mass for him to-morrow, and then she reached her own house. M. Rison was standing at the door ready to welcome her, and the large kitchen, with its rich old china, its great fire, cheerful lamps, and well-spread supper-table looked very inviting indeed.

"Run, young one," the farmer said. "Run upstairs and change thy wet things. If thou hadst not come within the next five minutes I should have sallied forth to meet thee."

Then M. Rison closed the door and drew the bolts, and shut out the murkiness of the night, the falling snow, and the bitter, wintry wind.

The gleam of firelight which had shone out when the farmer held the door open had looked pleasant enough—at least, so thought a young man who stood in the lane. He heard the sounds of the bolts, and then directly afterwards the chimes of the church clock striking nine, and then the strokes of the *De profundis* bell.

"Three hours before the *diligence* would start," he thought! And there was no shelter for him anywhere in that quiet town, because his pride prevented his humiliating himself, and because he believed still in the cause of the people. He went back along the lane, back by the castle and up the Grande Rue, and watched the rays that came through the chinks of the shutters in the house of the Mère Gilette, and when they were extinguished returned again to the quiet lane, and looked up at M. Rison's dwelling.

Behind one of those upstairs windows a young girl was sleeping in her neat little bed, while above her head the white Christ hung upon His Cross. The watcher knew the window; long ago she had told him which was her room. Had he been a fool? But it was too late now to think of that. It is easy enough to join secret societies and revolutionary bands, but it is not so easy to disassociate oneself from them. Jean knew that now. He stood out there in the snow, feeling like some lost spirit permitted to return for a while to the scenes of past happiness. It was not till near midnight that he set out for the bridge, and hailed Vojon as the heavy *diligence* rumbled over it. The old man recognized him as the same traveller who had made the afternoon journey. He could not see his face; he wore a scarf, and his hat was pulled low over his brow.

"A curious customer," the old man thought, and gathering up the reins called to his horses.

As long as a single light of the quiet hamlet remained in sight, the solitary traveller gazed forth. Then he covered his face with his hands.

"Too late," he whispered, "too late! and, O my God, we might have been so happy!"

CHAPTER VIII.

NOT a mile from where the great Cathedral of B—— towers up to its wonderful height, there was trouble in those bitter December days of which I write. The whole of the small hamlet was given up to an uneasy state of excitement. The mines were closed, and the hundreds of hands were out on strike. It was a period of wretchedness. The children were crying out for bread, in many of the cottages there was no fire, and groups of women, with their poor little ones round them, were sitting in a state bordering on despair. Out of doors the miners congregated, and spoke in low voices, while on their faces was a look of dogged resolution. They would not give in. Yesterday had been their last chance, M. Blondel, the owner of the mines, had said. He had come over in his carriage from his house near the village where the Mère Gilette lived, and made his last offer. He had offered to concede the original demand made by his men but three weeks ago, both as to an increase of wages, and a shortening of hours in the day's work, but it was refused. Since that demand, things had changed.

Some of the communistic leaders in Paris had taken the matter up, and had sent down a new scheme for improving the position of the miners. It is not necessary that I should trouble my reader with the details of this scheme. Sufficient to say that the proposals were preposterous, and such as no owner of the works was ever likely to listen to for an instant. But the men had had their heads turned. The Citizen Dobert had sent down his own right-hand man to do all he could to prevent the miners giving way, and so far, Jean had succeeded.

"I will wait here in the office for three hours," M. Blondel had said at the conclusion of his speech, "so as to give you all time to consider your position. I grant you your original demands, though I do not consider them really fair ones; still the times are exceptional, provisions are dear, and I am willing to meet you. But this new scheme I will not even consider. Remember, this is your chance. If you elect to throw it aside, you will only have yourselves to blame for it. For three hours, I say, I will wait. At the end of that time I shall return home, and instruct my secretary to enter on proposals which have already been made to me by Belgian and Flemish workmen, who are willing to come here and carry on the work, not on the new terms which I am offering to you, but on those old terms which you deem insufficient."

M. Blondel had gone back to the office after that speech, and with his secretary, the manager of the mines, and one or two foremen, had remained in anxious consultation. Outside, in the dark winter's afternoon, the miners had held grave debate. Some few were for giving in. Anxious wives and mothers of hungry families did their best to get them to do so, but it was useless. Jean carried out the instructions he had received; he pointed out to the men that subscriptions were coming in fast from all parts of the world from socialistic societies, and advised them to hold out. He made several speeches, but they were wanting in much of their old fire; still they had their effect, and before M. Blondel's carriage came out of the stable, and drew up at the doors of the bureau, they had elected to fight the fight out on the new demands.

It had been an anxious moment when the little group came out, carrying cash-boxes and account-books. It took some time to stow all that was wanted in the carriage, and during that time the men had gathered round and stood in front of the horses. Then M. Blondel and his attendants entered the carriage, and a great angry roar came from the miners. The safety of the occupants was probably due to the courage of M. Blondel. He stood up, and, holding a revolver in his hand, declared that he would shoot the first man who attempted to stop the horses, and then called to his coachman to proceed. At the same instant, the manager, the secretary, and the two foremen, had shown that they also had pistols in their hands, and the men, not liking the look of it, fell back. But as the carriage rolled along on its way, angry shouts were raised, and threats and curses were heard on all sides.

"Bring your Belgians here," they cried, "and we will kill them! Attempt to work your mines with other hands, and we will break up your machinery and destroy your shafts!"

M. Blondel sat motionless as one who heard not, holding his revolver ready for use. As soon as they were clear of the cottages, he called to the driver to whip up the horses, and to drive straight to the house of the Mayor of B———. In less than an hour the *gendarmes* had arrived at the mines and occupied the bureau, and placed guards at the different shafts. Then when he knew all was safe, M. Blondel had driven away along the white roads, through the frost and the snow, to his large, ugly house beyond the quiet little town where the Mère Gilette dwelt.

It was a bitter cold afternoon the day which followed the capitalist's offer to his men. Generally when the snow is once down it is warmer, but it had been lying now for weeks, while the sky overhead was of a dull, leaden colour, showing there was more still to come, and the bitter north-east wind howled across the land, and waved the bare branches of the trees wildly to and fro, while every piece of water for miles and miles around was frozen hard.

And so there was misery in the mining village near the old cathedral city. To be without food or fuel in such a frost as that was terrible. The women drew the children closer to them as they shivered in their cheerless dwellings, and tried to hush the wail that hunger every now and then raised. Occasionally the door of a cottage would be thrown open, and a great miner would enter to look for a pipe, may be, or tell of some new rumour of what was proposed, but as a rule they were but coldly received. From the first, the women had been for giving in. What was the use of attempting to fight in the midst of the cold of winter? It was madness. So they had shrieked and gesticulated, but it was of no avail. Jean had gone from platform to platform, and told the miners that money would come to enable them to hold out for their just demands, and they would not listen to the prudential reasons of their wives and daughters. But the thing which had caused the greatest breach of all in the camp was the rejection by the men of their own proposals. The women, who had to listen day and night to the cry of the shivering children demanding bread, were driven wild by this refusal. Food and drink, and fire, and an opportunity of putting by a few sous each week—all this had been in their very hands, so to speak, and they had cast it aside. And now—now it was said that in a few days foreign workmen would come, and take the place of the former labourers, and what would be done then? There was nothing left, the women wailed, but to die of hunger and cold.

"We shall have some money by and by," Guillot Gavot said to his wife as he entered his dwelling a little before dusk on the afternoon in question. Gavot was a miner who had been well to the front in urging the men to listen to Jean, and hold out. "The train which stops here at five o'clock from Paris is to bring it. The good Dobert, who sent the young fellow down, wrote this morning to him to say it would be here at that time—that he would send it by the hand of a man he could trust."

The woman raised her head, which had been

resting on her hands. She was sitting before the empty hearth on which lay a few dead embers which had long ago burnt themselves out, and huddled near her were three children looking the picture of misery.

"What matter?" she answered, shrugging her shoulders. "Are you so foolish as to think that this can go on for long—that folks will give money to keep you in idleness?"

"So long as *he* holds out, they will," Gavot answered roughly. He had thought she would have been pleased to hear the news, and was irritated that it had not had that effect. "So long as that. Jean Gilette has told me so a dozen times."

"And when these Belgians come, how then?" his wife asked sarcastically.

"Pah! Do you think for an instant that that was anything but a threat? Blondel thought to frighten us. Belgians, indeed! Come here and take the bread out of *our* mouths! Do you think any Belgian or other foreigner would dare to do that? We would kill them long before they got up here from the station!"

The woman did not reply. She let her head fall on to her hands again, and took no further notice of her husband. Gavot stood by the window, drumming his fingers against the glass.

Well, he had meant to bring her good news, but if she chose to receive it like that, she might. Then he put his hands in his pocket, and felt that there were still a few sous left. He had meant to keep those to buy a little bread for supper, but now as this money was coming from Paris, he need not trouble about that. And then, if she chose to take on so when he was but fighting for her and her children to make them better off, she did not deserve that he should deny himself the comfort of a drink and a little tobacco. Gavot went out, jingling the sous, down to the little *café*, where they sold vile brandy and still viler absinthe.

The time wore on. Down in the valley they could see from the mining village that the porters were lighting the signal lamps. It only wanted half an hour to the time when the slow train from Paris would stop at the little station. Already groups of men were wending their way down there, though it was well known that the actual distribution of the relief money would take place at a large shed near the principal shaft of the mine. A hastily constructed platform had been arranged, and a deal table placed thereon. Jean Gilette, it was said, assisted by his friend from Paris, would commence distributing the money there punctually at six o'clock.

Gavot went into the little *café*, and had some of the vile brandy, which did not tend to put him in a much better humour. He spent the remaining sous in the purchase of some tobacco, and sat arguing with other miners as to what the probable amount to each man would be. There were seven hundred and twenty-seven hands out on strike. It would want nearly four thousand francs to give five francs to each man. They must have that at least. All their savings had gone. It was a fortnight since the actual strike began. Some of the men inclined to think that it would be more a great deal than that— quite ten francs a piece, but Gavot thought not. The tobacco had put him in a little better humour. He should be quite content with the five francs, he said. And then, as it was nearly time for the train to arrive, the group of workmen drained their glasses, and prepared to descend to the station. They would be back after six for another drink, they called out to the proprietor of the *café*, and went off down the hill laughing.

It was quite dark when at five o'clock the little telegraph bell announced that the train had left the station before the one situated at the mines. It was only four and a half kilometres off. It would not be long now. The station-master locked the door leading on to the platform to keep out the crowd, but it was of no avail. In less than a minute the door was forced, and some two or three hundred miners fought their way through the little bureau, out on to the platform. Far away in the distance they could see the red lights in front of the engine. The train would soon be in. There was Gilette ready to receive his friend. The men crowded round, patting him on the back and cheering him, and while they were so engaged, the horn sounded and the train steamed slowly into the station. A minute or two later, and Jean saw a youth whom he had known in Paris struggling towards him carrying a box. Quickly seizing one end of it, the pair fought their way through the miners, and started up the hill at a run followed by the crowd, roaring and shouting like a pack of hungry wolves. There was no time to ask what amount had been brought, or even to speak a word. They were afraid that some of the rougher lot might seize on the spoil, and so made their way to the shed with all possible speed.

It was only with the greatest difficulty that Jean and his companion struggled up on to the platform, for the shed was already filled to overflowing, and their coats were nearly torn off their backs as they made their way through the throng. An oil lamp or two were passed up to them, and Jean pulled forth his list. Every man was to come singly on the platform, he said, receive his share, and sign his name, or put his mark against his name on the roll which had been prepared.

"There are seven hundred and twenty-seven men," Jean remarked. "How much have you brought with you? Be quick, so that we may see how much there is for each man."

Gilette's companion looked at him in rather a frightened way, and said, "Dobert has not received the amounts promised yet. Half the cheques and bills have had to be returned for endorsements and other formalities. He will send some more money to-morrow, and then you are to explain to the men that for the future they will be paid once a week, always at the end of the week. Dobert did not want to send any money till he is able to make an allowance of twenty-five francs a week per man, and he bids me say he only sends this instalment because you pressed him for money."

"Pressed him! *Nom de Dieu!*" exclaimed Jean, "how does he expect the men to live without money? They have had no wages for a fortnight! How much does the box contain?"

"It was all in silver, a little over two thousand francs," was the reply.

"*Nom de Dieu!*" Jean exclaimed again, and went to work with his pencil. It was a little over two francs and a half per man, he found.

"More will be sent to-morrow," he explained. "The good Dobert will, after that, pay it out every Saturday. He talks of allowing you at the rate of twenty-five francs per week, but for my part, I cannot think he is likely to have so much in hand, even though he states that the money is coming from all parts of the world."

"Twenty-five francs a week! That was good enough," the men said. There had been an angry outcry at the smallness of the sum after wasting all this time, but the knowledge that more was expected to-morrow, and that afterwards they would be allowed at the rate of twenty-five francs a week, mollified them.

The meeting broke up after the distribution. Most of them set out at once for the old cathedral city, there to buy provisions, and to return in haste to their families. Others despatched their wives or children on the errand, and took themselves off to drink at the little *café*. When, long after midnight, the proprietor put out the lights and closed the doors, he did not go to bed. Like the wise and prudent man that he was, he waited another half-hour till all was still, and then in spite of the cold and the snow, he walked over to B—— and awakened his brother, leaving with him all the money he had taken that day to be lodged safely the next morning at the bank. He had not been born yesterday, the proprietor remarked, as he bade his brother good-night, and set off home again. He understood making hay while the sun shone, and was careful of the stacking of such hay.

The next afternoon the same train brought another box of money containing about the same amount, but the day following, none arrived. There was an account of the strike in some of the journals, and large sums were named as having been sent from socialists in London, Belgium, and parts of Germany. Jean made a calculation of the amounts mentioned, and found that they came to a very large sum indeed. He telegraphed to the Citizen Dobert to let them have some money as soon as possible. Accordingly, the next afternoon, the youth who had come from Paris before, and whose name was Fausset, arrived with another box. This time there was more money—nearly four francs for each man, but this did not satisfy. Every Saturday, they had been told, they were to receive the sum of twenty-five francs; this was Saturday, and all they received was a miserable four francs! "What was the meaning of it?" the men cried, and gathered round the platform with angry faces and terrible oaths. Jean told them that he, too, had understood that that sum would be distributed that day. If he had not thought so, he would not have gone about giving counsel to hold out, and not to make overtures to M. Blondel, as some of the miners in their wretchedness had been proposing lately. He would telegraph at once to Dobert. There was some mistake. No doubt, in a couple of hours, probably less, they would learn how it had arisen.

Dobert sent a reply in much less than two hours. He had thought that Jean had understood that the distributions at the rate of twenty-five francs a week would begin, not that Saturday, but the following one. To avoid inconvenience, Dobert would send a small box early in the coming week, and then the large sum would be despatched on Saturday by the train which left the Gare du Nord at four o'clock in the morning, so that the money could be distributed soon after mid-day. Jean was very sorry for the men's disappointment. He told them so, and they believed him.

"It must have been my careless way of reading what he wrote," he said to some of the leaders. He was vexed. It seemed as if he were to blame. Then his thoughts wandered away to his home, nineteen kilometres off. In the darkness and the snow he had gone there once, when first he came to the mining village, but he would not go again. He had seen it all—the place familiar to him since his birth—and felt that he loved it now as he had never loved it in the old days. He had stood outside his mother's house, and he had followed Babette home through the snow. As he had stood watching the rays through the chinks of the shutter, he had ventured to press it back a little, in the hopes of seeing the room he knew so well, but he had failed; and suddenly the door of the house had opened, and she had come forth, and he had followed her—the girl of his choice, the girl who had once been his betrothed, whom he had loved, loved far more dearly than he had ever known. He had found that out long ago in the wretchedness of his Paris life.

No, he would not go to the village again. It would tempt him to desert his cause—the cause of the poor. And yet, how he longed to return! even to find himself labouring once more with honest Turquin, in the dark old forge, where the blowers roared, and the sparks flew up the chimney, while outside the river rolled softly, silently along beneath the stone bridge. Had kind, honest old Turquin ever given him a thought, he wondered? He had hated the work when he was at it, but now he thought that it was far preferable to that which now engaged his time. No, he thought Turquin would not quite have forgotten him.

And Babette! Had she? he wondered. Perhaps already she was betrothed to some one else! Very likely the night he had seen her come out from his mother's cottage she had gone there to tell her of it. The thought disturbed him. Babette —his Babette, belonging to any one else! He could not bear it. Pah! what a fool he was! What was the use of dreaming thus? With his own hands he had deliberately cut himself adrift from the homely life—from the quiet village, the grey old church, the forge, Turquin, M. le Curé—above all, from his mother and Babette. He had given them up to satisfy the restlessness and ambition of youth. He had adopted a cause, it was true, and served it faithfully, but it was not for the people that he had originally abandoned what had once been his. He knew that now; he recognized that it was *self* that had led him apart from the ties which had held him to his Norman home—self and pride: to be different from those who were content to toil and pray.

And this cause, did he still believe in it?

Partly. He no longer believed that all those who had wealth forgot the wretchedness of their poorer brethren. The Abbé Larmé had proved that to him. He thought of the ladies he had seen at their work in those slums of Paris; above all, he remembered the face of the beautiful Sicilian princess, with the silvery voice which reminded him of Mdlle. Laure. How he would like to see again the grey walls and the pointed turrets of that beautiful *château* where, in his childish days, it had been his greatest pleasure to be taken by his mother. How well he knew those beautiful corridors, those great rooms with their white and gold furniture, about which he had been allowed to roam while his mother went to speak with Madame la Duchesse. The other night, in the midst of the snow, he had passed the iron gates, and had gazed out of the window of the *diligence*, trying to get a sight of the place, but it had been too dark. He was sorry for that. He would like to have seen it again. Now he would never do so, he told himself. When his work at the mining village was over he would have to go back to Paris— back to the Citizen Dobert, and the club meetings, and all that he was getting to hate.

The days went by. The cold, which had

abated for a little, returned with renewed vigour. The box of money arrived on the Tuesday, but still there was great wretchedness. Long before Friday the money was exhausted, and in the houses there was neither food nor fire. Hunger is bad—it breeds ill-feeling. Brawls were of hourly occurrence. Wives were continually upbraiding their husbands. The children were wailing for bread. There was no food, no fire— nothing. And on Thursday a rumour came, a terrible rumour that M. Blondel's negotiations were all but concluded, and that before very long the Belgian and Flemish workmen would come to take their places at the mines. At the very same hour, too, as the tale became rife, a large force of *gendarmes* made their appearance and took up their residence in the various sheds round the shafts. The other force had been quite inadequate to cope with the miners had any real attempt been made to damage the workings. Now it was felt it would be useless. It was a strong force, sufficient even to protect the foreigners when they should come.

To Jean it was a terrible time. It seemed as if the days would never go, as if Saturday would never come. There was a bad feeling amongst some of the men, too, against him. They treated him as if he was responsible, he declared, for

Dobert's delays. On Friday, things had reached such a pitch that an offer was made to him of shelter in one of the sheds by an officer of the *gendarmes*. He declined: he would not, indeed, hear of it. "As he pleased," was the answer. His safety, they told him, must be his own lookout then.

At last Saturday came, the day which was to see the great boxes of money arrive by the midday train. Jean rose with a feeling of thankfulness. Only four hours to wait, he thought, as he passed the *café*, and caught a glimpse of the clock within. Involuntarily as he did so, he turned, and looked down the hill towards the little station. A man in a blouse was coming up the road, and as he saw Jean he held up his arm and waved a paper. It was a telegram, no doubt, to say the money had been despatched.

He went down the hill, and met the messenger. Yes, he was right. It was a telegram. He thanked the man, who turned to go back rather hurriedly, he thought, and retracing his steps, Jean tore open the envelope, and read:

Paris, December 17th. Seven o'clock.
Dobert missing for last forty-eight hours—has absconded with the whole of the money received—left nothing—whereabouts unknown—supposed to have gone to Spain.—LETIER.

The earth seemed to spin round and round to Jean as he read the words. There was a noise in his ears like the noise of a train. He tried to walk, but he staggered like a drunken man, and had to lean for support against a tree. What was he to do? What could any one do? The men would kill him, that was certain. They would tear him to pieces like wild beasts in their madness. And they had left him to face it alone—those cowards with whom he had worked so long in Paris—left him alone to be lynched by the furious mob which would seize on him in their despair. Well, a man could die but once. He would die at the hands of the people he had thought to serve.

The minutes went by. After a while he grew better. The earth ceased to whirl round and round. He stood up and took a breath, and found that his lips were wet, and passing his hand across them discovered that it was with blood. His mouth was full of it, too. It was the shock, he supposed. Well, anyhow, he must go and tell the men, and just as he thought this, he heard steps, and looked up. It was a couple of *gendarmes*, and one of them was the officer who had offered him shelter. They stopped and asked what ailed him. He could not answer; he only held out the telegram. The officer read it, and as he did so, his face grew very serious.

"There will be trouble," he said.

Jean nodded. It was difficult to speak. The position of the people paralyzed him. Without food, money, or employment, their places taken by foreign workmen, and he the one who had given counsel again and again to hold out! He looked at the dull leaden sky indicating more snow, and then at the cottages round. Not from a single chimney could he see any smoke.

"There will be trouble," the *gendarme* said again. "It will be better for you to accept shelter with us. You will have to make it known. We will come with you to the platform."

But Jean refused. He would not be the first to show mistrust of the people.

"Let them kill me," he said, "I do not care—at least, very little. It will soon be over. I am so tired of it all. And then, though it is not my fault really, I feel as if I were to blame. I will go. It is better to get it over."

It was not yet nine, and though in France the hours are far earlier than in England, there were not many people about. What was the use of rising before there was need, the people asked? Besides, lying quiet, you felt the pangs of hunger and cold less. As Jean passed through the principal street of the mining village he met only three people. The last of them was one of the leaders of the men. His face was white, and there was an evil look on his countenance. He, too, held a paper in his hand. He glanced at Jean and said: "You have heard it. I can see that. Did he send to you also? But we will kill them—if they come."

"If who come?" Jean asked.

"These men. I thought by your face he had written to you also. Blondel has written to tell me the negotiations are concluded, and that the men will be here next week—that all the places have been filled."

"*Mon Dieu!*" was all that Jean could say. Then he handed the telegram to the man, who read it. They did not speak—only stood there in silent horror at the whole position. Jean was the first to break the silence.

"I am going to the platform. Will you spread it about?—the news I mean. I will wait for them there."

"They will kill you," was the answer.

"Very likely. And yet, yet it is not my fault. I meant to do my best for them. How could I know that Dobert was evil as Judas?"

"I do not blame you," the other answered. "I believe you, but the others will not. When men are mad with hunger and despair they want to tear and rend something. It will be so with you. I am sorry. Give me your hand."

Jean did so. "Tell them," he said, "that I was true to them, I mean after they have killed me. The *gendarmes* offered to protect me, but I would not have it so. I would not be the first to mistrust them. My life is in their hands." Then he went on towards the platform and the shed, while the man he had spoken to went down the little street.

It was very still. Jean, when he drew near the waste ground which surrounded the shed, seated himself on the trunk of a fallen tree and waited. Now and then a flake of snow fell, and mechanically his eyes followed its flight. Then he turned and looked towards the little town, scarce a mile off, with the mighty Cathedral towering upwards, and then on to the distant hills. Beyond those hills was his home, his mother, Babette! Then the stillness was broken. There was a noise. The people were coming. He was going to die.

He turned to enter the shed. If he mounted the platform he might be able to speak to them, to tell them that it was not his fault, to tell them that he had been true to them, and as he thought this, he found himself seized, and in a moment discovered that he was in the hands of the *gendarmes*. He struggled to free himself, but it was useless, while they protested it was for his own safety. They closed round him at the very moment that an immense mass of miners were seen approaching at a run. He called out to them to rescue him, but it was of no avail. The *gendarmes* retreated towards their own quarters, carrying him with them, but as he was borne backwards he heard the shrieks of fury, the cries of "traitor," "robber," saw the savage faces that glared at him, and the eager arms that tried to snatch him from the grasp of the police. They wanted to get at him, to kill him, they cried. Then a stone struck him on the head, and he knew no more.

It was noon when Jean opened his eyes in a wooden out-house, and wondered where he was. Then his glance fell on a *képi* and a blue coat hanging on a nail near, and he remembered also what had happened. In the next shed he could hear the rattle of plates and the sound of voices. It was some of the *gendarmes* breakfasting. There seemed a great discussion going on. He sat up and listened.

"Happen what may," said a voice, "I have carried out my instructions. If I had followed the men, I should not have done so. My orders were to protect the mines, and I have no authority to leave them, even for an hour. Besides, it is my belief that they are far too exhausted to get as far as Blondel's *château*. Why, it is beyond G——, and that is nineteen kilometres if it is a foot."

"If they reach it they will certainly burn it down in their present temper," some one else replied. "The men are mad. I should not wonder if they fire, not only Blondel's *château*, but the whole of G——, because he lives there."

"Possibly," the first voice answered, and then there was a silence, broken only by the rattle of the plates and the knives and forks.

G—— threatened—and in a way through him! Jean's heart seemed to stop beating at the mere thought. The men were mad. It was quite true. He remembered their faces, their curses, everything. And his mother and Babette were there! It was impossible to say what might not happen. He must go to them to help them. If he made a noise, the *gendarmes* would hear and prevent him. He looked round to see if there was any way of escape, and noticed that the board close to the spot where he lay was quite loose. If he gave it a push it would go, and then he could drop out at the back of the shed and be free of the enclosure in which the *gendarmes* were encamped. He bent the wood back gently and with ease, and then slid softly out. The nails at the other end of the board still held it, so he pushed it back into its place and began to descend the hill, taking care to avail himself of every bush as a cover, in case any of the *gendarmes* should be about. In a few minutes he was out of sight of the mining village, and making his way across the fields in the direction of G——.

It was some time before Jean thought it safe to venture out on the high road, for fear any of the mounted *gendarmes* should be patrolling there; but at length he emerged about four kilometres from the mining village, and began as rapid a progress as he could, taking care, however, to keep close to the hedge on the left, so that if any blue coats made their appearance he could slip through into a place of safety.

It was only with difficulty that Jean was able to keep on at the rate he did. His head ached and throbbed, and now and then the same sensation as if the ground was whirling round, compelled him to pause. But he fought his way onward. He would do what he could to save those he loved, if there was danger. He did not know how long it was since the mob had started

—knew, indeed, nothing save the desire to get on. By and by he came to a small village, and saw that something unusual had happened. Women and children were looking out of their cottage windows with frightened faces, and men were standing about in groups, talking. The windows of a *café* had been broken, and the ground was strewn with glass, while it was evident from the appearance of the inside that the place had been wrecked. The unhappy owner was sitting on a bench in front of the door, looking the very picture of misery. He would be ruined he said, over and over again, to those who tried to comfort him.

Jean's appearance naturally excited some remark. His head had been bandaged, while he was unconscious, by one of the *gendarmes*, but it had been roughly done, and the handkerchief was soaked through with blood. His clothes had been torn in the endeavours made to keep him from the hands of the mob, and his head was bare. Then some one spoke, and asked if he had been ill-treated, and he answered that the men had been mad, and did not know what they were doing. "Was it long since they had passed through the village?" he asked. Not more than an hour or so, was the reply. They had wrecked the *café*, and gone on half-mad with drink.

They were going to the *château* of M. Blondel, it was said. Then Jean went on along the road to G——.

The time wore on. An hour ahead of him! Whenever he thought of it, he ran—ran till he could run no further, and it seemed to him as if his heart would burst. It was nearly four o'clock when he topped the hill, and looked down at G——, lying at his feet. He could see beyond the ruined castle the chimneys of M. Blondel's new mansion. There was no smoke nor fire. The sight gave him courage. He should be in time to be beside his mother and Babette if any danger threatened them. He fled on till he reached the outskirts of the village he knew so well. The ivy-covered walls of the Château de Mérillac were in sight. People were standing out in the road just as he had noticed in the village through which he had passed some time back; they were not looking towards the little town, but away to the left, towards the entrance to the *château*. Jean's eyes followed the direction of theirs. The iron gates had been forced from their hinges, and were lying on the ground.

"What is it?" he asked a woman. She was a stranger to him.

"The miners," she answered. "The men from beyond B——, who had been on strike.

It was thought when they were seen coming, that they would attack the house of M. Blondel, but there was some mistake. A cry was raised that this was the *château*, and in a moment the gates were torn down. The men were mad. It was feared they would burn the house of Madame la Duchesse over her head."

Jean did not answer. For a moment he stood speechless. The *château* he had known from his childish days—threatened through his fault, through his folly! He must save it, but how—how—how? To go up under the avenue would be death. They would tear him in pieces. It would be of no avail. If he could reach the *château* he might speak to them from a window, from one of the turrets. Then suddenly there flashed on him the remembrance of the stables which lay at the back, and which he could reach by a lane a little higher up to the left. And as the thought came to him, he started off running. People standing about got out of his way. He took no heed of them, and in less than five minutes he was at the gates. They were closed. He called, but there was no answer. He could hear the shouts of the mob in front, the cry for Blondel.

"The fools! the idiots!" Jean thought. There was no time to be lost. Somehow he scaled the walls, and let himself down into the courtyard and got into the house. He made his way through the outer offices without meeting any of the servants. He could hear the furious shouts of the mob. He fled on, reached the door of the long gallery which led towards the vestibule, and, as his steps echoed on the stairs, he heard cries. A moment later, and he flung open the door. Some women servants who were there screamed at sight of him, and then his eyes fell on the tall stately figure of Madame de Mérillac, who was standing with some one a little apart from the group, waiting for whatever might happen, waiting calmly, as did those of her blood in the days of old in the Salle des Pas Perdus. Then the figure who stood near turned, and Jean was face to face with his mother. With a cry she waved him back, and strove to put herself between him and Madame Mérillac. In an instant he divined what she believed—that it was he who was leading the mob against the house of her beloved mistress. He strove to tell her, to undeceive her; but even as he opened his lips to speak, he saw the face that he had longed to see and kiss again horribly distorted by the convulsive workings of the muscles on the left side, and then with a shriek the Mère Gilette fell paralyzed and unconscious at the feet of the mistress she loved, and whom she was seeking to protect.

CHAPTER IX.

"Back!"

Madame de Merillac spoke the word as Jean tried to lift his mother from the ground. She put out her hand, and waved him from the prostrate figure.

"I will tend her. My servants will help me. As for you, be satisfied with what you have done. Go back to your friends. Lead them to other parts of the *château* first. It will take some time to destroy it all. Let her remain here. It will not be for long. I think the end is not far. But do not come near her! She has been my faithful friend and servant. You have killed her. Rest satisfied with that."

Jean did not answer. He saw that Madame, like his mother, thought that it was he who had brought the mob to attack the *château*, but he could not explain. For the second time that day he heard again the roaring in his ears, and once more his mouth filled with blood. Outside, he could hear the shouts of the mob, and a loud hammering on the great door. Though the long gallery in which they stood seemed to whirl round and round, he knew that he must act if he would save the house from destruction. There was not a minute to lose. If he went out through the entrance, it would be instant death. He would have no time to speak to the people; besides, to open the door would be to admit the mob. He staggered to his feet, and put his hand to his head.

Then he remembered that from a window on the first floor of the left turret there was a little balcony. He would go there. If he offered himself to the people, perhaps they would spare the place. His own life he did not value. They would kill him because of what Dobert had done, but what did it matter after all? He looked down at the face of the Mère Gilette. It was all drawn and distorted. He had done that. It had been through a mistake—but still, it was his work. If he had never deserted her—never gone away to Paris, then it would not have been. Yes, it was his work after all. Then the shouts of the mob recalled him. He must go. He knelt down and kissed the paralyzed face very gently. Then he rose, and looked at Madame de Mérillac.

"You misjudge me," he said. "There is no time to explain now. I am going to try and save your house. I think I shall not come back. They have been misled, and think I am to blame.

They will kill me. If—if my mother should know anything again, say to her that I have longed night and day to look upon her face, and that I grieve for the pain I have given her. My pride is killed now. And see here, Madame, you are kind. I know it. If they kill me, will you tell Babette—she is the daughter of the good farmer Rison—will you tell her that I love her, that I have always loved her, in spite of whatever she may think?"

Then he bowed, and went along the gallery.

"Follow him," Madame de Mérillac said, turning to one of her footmen. "Jacques, you are a brave man. Follow him, I say, he may need your aid." Then she turned, and knelt down beside the Mère Gilette.

And outside, the mob thundered at the closed door and the shuttered windows.

Jean found the turret chamber in darkness. As he fumbled at the fastenings, some one came forward and assisted him. He did not know who it was. In another minute, the light of the winter's afternoon appeared, the window was opened, and the young man stepped forth.

A roar of anger broke from hundreds of throats as the eyes of the mob fell on Jean. How he came there they knew not, but the sight of him awoke their wrath. They believed that he had assisted Dobert in some way. That was enough. A great shout went forth to kill him, and the stones began to rattle round him. He stood alone there, facing them unmoved. After a while his calmness had its effect; the shouts died away, and they waited. He wished to speak, they said. Good, let him do so before he died.

"You think that I was false," he cried. "I do not blame you. Some day I believe that you will know I was innocent of any knowledge of the cruel wrong Dobert has done you—that I believed as truly as man can believe that the money would come by the mid-day train to-day. But enough. I know that you have reason to suspect me. But it is not of this that I would speak. Do not think that I shall fly from you. This morning I would have met you face to face to tell you the truth, but the *gendarmes* carried me off. I am ready to deliver myself up to you. I will do so, but tell me first, why are you here? This is not the house of M. Blondel. That is distant a mile off."

"We know it now," a voice answered. "We thought at first that this was it—some one said it was the *château*, and we came. No matter. It is the house of an aristocrat. We will destroy it first, and then pay Blondel our visit."

"But it is the house of one who has done you no wrong, of one who deals kindly with the poor and the sad. Why should you harm the house of Madame la Duchesse?"

"Because she is an aristocrat, I say," the other returned, "and aristocrats have for centuries lived on the blood of the people. We suffer, let her suffer, too. It is only fair. We will burn it down. They are vermin, these titled beings. There is nothing like fire when you deal with vermin."

They were his own words. Jean remembered them well—spoken in the club-room, and so much applauded, that the committee had ordered his speech to be printed and sent to be distributed wherever there were branches of the society. He turned sick and faint. He had sown the seed, and was now reaping the harvest. The words were caught up now, and he heard them pass from mouth to mouth. "There is nothing like fire when you deal with vermin." And then a shout arose—they were mad, these men—mad with hunger and disappointment, and drink stolen from the wretched *cafés* on the way from B——, and so, I say, a shout arose to fire the place—to fire it, "with the rats in it." Then in a moment a torch gleamed, and Jean knew there was but one chance left.

"Stay—stay," he cried. "Listen! I have a proposal to make. You think I have been a traitor, and traitors should die. If I come down and deliver myself to you, will you spare this place—the home of one who has done you no wrong, and whose name is known far and wide for the good she has done? Say, is it an agreement?"

They paused. In the failing twilight the torches swayed backwards and forwards, and savage faces glared up at him, but yet his words had an effect. To stand there alone and offer his life! It touched them.

"I am ready and willing to die to save this place," Jean said again, and would have gone on, would have pleaded, only a hand was laid upon his arm, and looking round, he saw Madame de Mérillac.

"Stay there," she said, speaking to some of her servants who had accompanied her and would have followed her from the room out on to the balcony. "Stay there. The stones might injure you." Then she looked at the mob and spoke.

"I have heard his words," she said, putting out her hand towards Jean. "He is a brave man. In the past he has erred, but words like those he has spoken wipe away many offences. My servants are here. At my orders they will prevent his descending among you. I will not save my house at the expense of a brave man's life. There are too few brave men in the world in these days for that. And I will not plead to you—as the widow of a de Mérillac, and as the daughter of the proudest marquis in all France, I will not plead. I have done you no wrong. To the best of my means I have striven to help always those who suffer, and now you surround my house and threaten it with destruction. Well, do your worst. I say again, I will not plead for myself or my property, but listen: this man who stands beside me, who has adopted your cause, who has been true and loyal to you—his mother but a few moments since was stricken with paralysis. Let her be removed in peace to a place of safety. In the past she served me faithfully, and she was with me when God took from me my husband and my only child. Let her, I say, be removed in safety. For myself I ask nothing."

She ceased to speak, and there was a murmur among the throng. They glanced upward at the tall, stately figure in black, with the silvery hair crowning her face, and there came a sort of awe upon them. She was a woman, and she was in their power. She had defied them—had told them that not even for the sake of her home would she condescend to plead to them, but her proud bearing, her bravery touched them. She stood there facing them—calm, motionless as a statue. Again there was a murmur. She had done them no wrong, she had striven to aid those who suffered or were sad. After all, it was Blondel they wanted. As for Jean, it seemed as if he had spoken the truth. Let it be as this aristocrat wished. She was a brave woman— she deserved something. Then one of the leaders of the men stepped forward and spoke. As he did so he stood uncovered.

"You have not pleaded, and it is true that you and your property are in our power, but you have done us no wrong. It is the Citizen Blondel whose house must be fired, not yours. We will do you no harm. As for Gilette, now that he speaks, we believe him. Rest satisfied, Madame; we retire, and leave you in peace. And—and see here—you are nothing to us; you scorn us as a mob, but when you said that just now about your husband and your child, we were sorry. It is not well to be alone like that. We understand. We are not so bad as you think."

Then the man bowed and ceased to speak, looking up at the balcony.

Madame de Mérillac endeavoured to reply,

and failed. The words addressed had profoundly moved her. She glanced at the gaunt faces on which hunger and wretchedness were written, and her heart was stirred within her. She turned to Jean. "Tell them that I thank them—tell them that I grieve for their misery. Say I wish to help them if I can, and that I would speak with their leaders."

Jean did as he was bid. There was no harm in complying with such a wish. Two or three men advanced towards the door, which was unbarred to admit them. Madame de Mérillac turned to re-enter the window, but before she did so, her eyes filled with tears at sight of the wretched crowd below in their want. Here and there a hat was lifted, and twice over she bowed her acknowledgments. Then she passed into the *château*, and went downstairs to receive the men. Jean would have gone to his mother, but the Duchesse bade him remain with her.

In the great drawing-room of the *château*, with its faded white and gold draperies and Louis Quatorze furniture, Madame de Mérillac received the leaders of the strike.

"Can nothing be done, can no terms be arranged?" she asked, when the position of affairs was placed before her. "Do not think I do not feel sorry for you. I feel for your disappointment, for your want on account of this cruel, this treacherous Dobert, but, my friends, you have been foolish. Why did you strike—why, when your own proposals were offered to you ?"

They could only plead that it was by Dobert's advice. They had believed him, and this was what had happened! And now their place had been filled up by Belgian and Flemish workmen. Revenge was all that was left to them. They would burn the house of the Citizen Blondel that night.

"I will have no threats," Madame de Mérillac answered. "And now, listen to me. Are you willing to undertake that the men remain quietly here while I visit M. Blondel? I think that perhaps I may be able to effect a compromise."

A compromise—when all chance of such a thing seemed past! The leaders seized eagerly on the proposal. Not a man should stir. To that they pledged their honour.

Five minutes later, and Madame de Mérillac entered her brougham by the back way, and drove through the frightened town to the newly-built mansion of M. Blondel. As she passed over the bridge, she caught a glimpse of M. le Curé waving to the driver to stop. She opened the door from the inside and signed to him to take a seat beside her. Then the carriage went on.

"I have been away over to N——, and I only returned just now, and was hurrying down to the *château*—for I heard that it was surrounded—to seek to aid you."

"There is nothing to be apprehended," Madame de Mérillac answered, and then briefly related what had passed.

Presently they drew up at the door of M. Blondel's new mansion.

"There is no time for ceremony," Madame de Mérillac said as she met the mine-owner in the hall, "so I will not apologize for intruding. My house was mistaken for yours, and has been in imminent danger from the miners. They were coming here to burn yours down over your head, but I have obtained a solemn promise from them not to stir till I return. I have promised to negotiate. M. Blondel, is there no possible chance of a compromise?"

"How, Madame?" the mine-owner asked, with a shrug of his shoulders. "I have done all I could. I offered them their own terms even, but they refused. A man in Paris, one Dobert by name—he is, I believe, well known to the authorities—is collecting money for them, and allowing them, I am told, twenty-five francs a week! Of course that cannot go on for long, but it has given them such confidence that they resisted all my endeavours, and now I have been driven to fill their place with foreign workmen. They will set out from Belgium in a few days."

"But you know what has happened concerning this man Dobert?"

"*Mille pardons*, Madame, but I know nothing beyond what I have stated," M. Blondel answered.

"He has fled—taken all the money with him; the men are starving—literally starving! He has deceived them; they have received nothing of what was collected save a few miserable francs. They are mad with hunger and cold, and despair."

"*Mon Dieu!* the poor fellows," M. Blondel said, for he had a kind heart. Then a door opened, and Madame Blondel appeared, and a few moments were lost while the mine-owner presented his wife to Madame de Mérillac, and related to her the position of affairs.

"Can nothing be done?" the latter asked when these formalities were over.

M. Blondel raised his shoulders to his ears and held out both his hands.

"What can Madame la Duchesse suggest?" he asked. "If I had not already engaged these foreigners, I would willingly take the men back on the old terms—they would be glad enough to return on them, I make no doubt, but I have contracted to pay these men their railway-fares, and engaged them for a term of not less than three weeks. I am not very rich, in spite of what folks believe. I have but lately finished this place. I can no more pay these foreigners their three weeks' wages, and take back the old hands also, than I can buy all Paris. It is impossible."

"How much would it cost to pay the foreigners?" Madame de Mérillac asked.

M. Blondel drew forth a pocket-book and began to make a calculation in it. "There are quite seven hundred foreigners engaged," he said; then he frowned, and worked away in silence for a few minutes. Then again he shrugged his shoulders. The thing could not be dreamt of, happen what might. The sum amounted to between three and four thousand pounds.

There was a silence in the large vestibule where M. Blondel, his wife, the Curé, and Madame la Duchesse stood. Outside the light had all but failed, and in the stillness they could hear the horses pawing the ground. Then the silence was broken. Madame de Mérillac spoke.

"They are very wretched—their little children and their wives are crying for bread. I am alone. God in His wisdom has taken from me those whom in old days I should have had to consider. I have much of this world's goods. M. Blondel, if you will take back your old hands, I will pay the foreigners this money. I am sorry for these poor starving men here. They have been misled. It is the *teachers* of revolutionary doctrines I blame, not their *dupes*."

There was a pause. M. Blondel could scarcely believe his ears, and stout Madame Blondel was so overcome that she had to sit down on a neighbouring chair.

Then M. le Curé spoke, half to himself. "They have been badly taught. It is the old tale—' They know not what they do.' It is a great sacrifice. Blessed be God, Who hath put it into the heart of Madame la Duchesse to do unto others as she would they should do unto her!"

Madame de Mérillac gently touched his arm, as though to recall this priest with the long dark hair, and the eyes that seemed to be gazing always into the future.

"Hush!" she said. "There is no sacrifice. I am rich, and I am alone. Why should I not do it?"

"Blessed be God!" M. le Curé said.

Then Madame de Mérillac spoke: "M. Blon-

M

del, you have not answered me. Will you do as I ask?"

"But, Madame, it is not fair to yourself. Great Heaven, such kindness—such generosity!"

"Tush, tush, *mon ami*," she broke in. "It is agreed then. Get into my carriage, and come back and speak to your men. Madame, believe me, your husband will be safe. In an hour he will return to you."

Madame Blondel burst into tears. She was fat, and she was vulgar, but her heart was warm. She took the hand that Madame de Mérillac held out to her.

"It is not that," she sobbed. "I know he will be safe now, but the fright—and you—you have been so good!" Then, in her gratitude, she kissed the hand she held, and went with them to the door.

"Have no fear—in an hour," Madame de Mérillac said as the door closed.

Then the carriage drove away across the green, past the little hotel, over the stone bridge, and so to the back entrance of the *château*.

"Are the leaders still here?" she asked of one of the servants, and learning that they were yet in the great drawing-room, went thither. A few wax tapers had been lighted, which seemed only to make the darkness more visible. The men rose as she entered. Then their eyes fell on M. Blondel, and they gave a little start. For a moment no one spoke. Then the mine-owner said:

"My friends, you have had a bad time," and then he stopped. He could not go on. He tried, but he failed. "It is the hungry look in their faces," he explained to M. le Curé, and turned away. The men saw it and were touched, and the one who stood nearest to M. Blondel held out his hand. The mine-owner took it and pressed it. Then he tried to speak, and again he failed.

"You tell them," he said to the priest.

The Curé came forward. As a rule, the miners did not like the clergy. They believed that the Church was in league with the upper classes to grind them down, but there was something about the kind face, the spare figure, that in spite of themselves attracted them. Then he began to speak, and in a little while—in a little while they understood—understood that he loved them—was glad at what he had to tell them—understood that he wanted to serve them.

"*Mes amis*," he said, "I have brought you good news. This lady here has asked M. Blondel to take you back, and he has consented. He is able to do this because Madame la Duchesse has undertaken to pay to the foreign workmen the whole of the three weeks' wages which is their due by the terms of the contract. It is a large sum, it amounts to about ninety thousand francs—she will do this, I say."

The Curé paused. The men stood silent, amazed, they could not speak. It was like a dream—ninety thousand francs! And but a few hours ago they had been about to burn her house over her head. The priest was about to continue, but M. Blondel, who had recovered his self-command, stepped in. He said that the Belgian workmen had agreed cheerfully to take the old scale of wages, and that as he had suffered loss, the men must understand that it was only at the lower rate of payment they returned. He could not allow Madame la Duchesse to do more than *lend* this large sum, and until he had repaid it he could not raise the wages. If, however, at the end of that time the men had worked cheerfully and well, he would grant the rise which they had originally asked for and in the end refused by the advice of the Citizen Dobert. Did they, speaking as leaders of the men, accept those terms?

They were beaten, utterly beaten. They had suffered so much, and all for nothing, worse than nothing! They had no fire, no food, they and their wives and children were starving. There was nothing else to do but to accept thankfully what they had before rejected. Then suddenly Madame de Mérillac spoke.

"*Mon ami*," she said, turning to M. Blondel, "these poor ones have suffered much. I do *not* lend this money. It is nothing to do with you. It is between myself and the miners that I pay off the foreigners, but in return I ask for them the immediate rise which you have promised at a future date."

M. Blondel bowed.

"I owe you too much to refuse, Madame," he said. Then he turned to the men.

"It is as Madame la Duchesse desires, you will tell the men. It is late, very late. You had better lead them back to their homes. But first, some of next week's wages must be paid in advance. To-morrow is Sunday, a day which M. le Curé here will tell you should be one of rest. It shall be so: a complete holiday. And as Madame la Duchesse has by her goodness and generosity made us all blush, I shall present to every man a double day's pay. If Madame will permit one of her footmen to go to my house, he will return with my secretary, who will bring to us some of the strong-boxes removed a few weeks back from the bureau."

In a few minutes a servant was despatched in the brougham. While he was absent, the leaders went out to carry the news to the men. In the drawing-room they could hear a sound like a great sob of joy which greeted its reception. The struggle was at an end. The cold and the hunger and the bitterness of the strike were things of the past.

And by and by the secretary returned, and the roll was called, and two days' wages paid to every man. It was M. Blondel's gift, the secretary said, as seated in the porch he distributed the much-needed money.

"Is it all over?" the mine-owner asked, when at about half-past six his secretary re-entered the drawing-room. "They will go now, I suppose."

But even as he spoke a shout arose, again and again renewed. The leaders of the strike returned. The people desired to express their thanks. Would it be too much to ask that M. Blondel would speak to them a few words from the turret balcony?

"It is not me, my friends, whom you should thank, it is the illustrious owner of this house to whom your gratitude is due."

"We wish to thank you both," the people said, and then a cry arose for Madame la Duchesse.

The night was dark, but the glare of the torches showed the slender figure in its deep mourning clearly, and as she stepped forth alone a great shout went up. Again and again it rose and fell.

"We thank you! We thank you! We thank you!"

Then there was a silence. And in the silence the Duchess spoke.

"Work well for your employer, and listen not to the counsels of evil men," she said. Then she turned and re-entered the room amidst the plaudits of seven hundred men. Jean was at the window and held back the curtain. In the torchlight they saw his face, and called to him to return, that they understood.

"May I speak to them, Madame?" he asked.

The Duchess bent her head.

Then the young man stepped out. "I will not return," he said. "I was loyal to you and you mistrusted me, but that is passed now. I have worked for you, but I think perhaps that I should have served you better had I listened to wiser teachers than those I served under in Paris. For my part, I have had enough of it all. My home is here in this village and here I shall remain." Then he stopped. His home! In a few hours he would not have one! He could not go on. They called to him, these people, that they were grieved, that they trusted him to the full. He must return with them. He should be *fêted*. In their excitement they had forgotten the illness of his mother.

"I thank you," he said, wearily, "believe me that I thank you; but I will not come. And if, if you think that I have any claim upon you for your misjudgment of me, will you show it now by going quietly away? My mother is dying here. In a little while it will be over, so they say. They tell me that she does not hear, but as I watched a while ago, it seemed to me as if she moaned when you shouted. So I should wish that it might be quiet. I think then that it will make the end easier for her. Do you see?"

They did not answer him, these men whom he had sought to serve, these men gaunt with hunger; but in a little while they began to withdraw, each man treading softly as though within the precincts of a sick-room, and as they filed past the turrets, they lifted their caps to him. They had treated him badly, ungratefully, and now he was in sorrow. So they saluted him. It could do him no good, but it was all they could do. Jean understood, and his eyes filled with tears. He stood there until the tramp of the seven hundred men died away in the distance, and the *château* was silent once more in the darkness of the winter's night. Then he heard the voice of Madame la Duchesse.

"Jean!" she said.

And Jean, hearing, understood.

CHAPTER X.

"Is it the end?"

Jean asked the question in the long, dim gallery, with his hand on the door of the room in which his mother lay.

"I do not know; I think so. The doctor deemed it advisable that M. le Curé should afford her the consolations of religion, he would not say for certain. They never will, these men of science," Madame de Mérillac answered.

Then together they entered the room.

The Mère Gilette was lying on a couch, breathing rather heavily. In the faint light of the candles it seemed to Jean that the left side of the face was less drawn. He did not know, but he fancied so. There was no one else in the apartment save one of Madame's maids, who had been keeping watch. The doctor had gone. He would not return till the next morning.

"It is a case for M. le Curé, not for me. He may accomplish more than I can," the little man said, with a bow. Unlike the general run of practitioners in France, the doctor was not an infidel. On the contrary, he was a very devout Christian, and never absent from his place at Mass on Sundays and *fêtes*.

Jean was about to advance to the bedside, but Madame made him a little sign to keep out of sight while she herself drew near. She took the hand of her old servant and gently stroked it. By and by the Mère Gilette opened her eyes and looked up. There was a glimmer of knowledge in the dark eyes which had known so much sorrow. She recognized her old mistress and tried to smile, but the left side was still too much drawn. It was only with difficulty that Jean could forbear a cry of pain. As it was, the quick ears of Madame la Duchesse caught the smothered groan. He did not speak, it is true, but who shall dare say that it was not an act of contrition in the sight of the Most High? Madame de Mérillac gave him a look of compassion.

"It is less than it was, I think," she whispered. "And then, there is no pain, that is so much, is it not?"

The weary eyes of the Mère Gilette had closed again. She did not appear to notice the voices.

"It is so much, *that*, is it not?" Madame de Mérillac said again. With Laure it had been so terrible, the fever, the thirst, the intense weakness and weariness. The Mère Gilette was going, but she was going very peacefully. Jordan's flood was bearing her away full gently. She had suffered all her life; perchance some special charge had been given on high by the Great King concerning this passing. Who shall say? All her life she had striven to serve Him, had bowed her head when in His wisdom He had afflicted her. He does not desert in their hour of need those who have kept close to Him. He is with them, depend upon it, in the darkness of the valley of the shadow of death.

The *château* was very still now. Only a few hours ago the shouts of a furious mob had echoed round the grey walls, but now all was hushed. Madame de Mérillac glanced at the little time-piece on the mantel-shelf and made a sign to the maid. On a small *priedieu* some candles were standing, and these were now lighted, and then the silent watch recommenced. It was nearly nine o'clock before the door-bell rang forth, the sound echoing in the intense stillness. There was a stir then in the room, a preparation, a pause, and then the door was opened and steps were heard in the passage, and the low murmur of Latin words. In the sick-chamber all sank on their knees as M. le Curé entered—M. le Curé with the sallow face and ugly features and long black hair, but somehow he did not look ugly. There was a light on his face just then. Perchance like Moses of old, his countenance reflected back the light of the Lord of glory Whom he bore. At least, so Madame de Mérillac thought, as the priest placed the Sacred Host upon the little altar, praying aloud as he did so that peace might be in that house and with all that dwelt therein. A moment later, and in the hush of the death-chamber fell the sacred words of the ritual: *Accipe, soror, Viaticum Corporis Domini nostri Jesu Christi, qui te custodiat ab hoste maligno, et perducat in vitam æternam. Amen.*

And then silence followed and the Mère Gilette had made her last Communion. Never any more on feast-days, when the bells were sounding for early Mass, would the door of the little cottage open and the Mère Gilette go forth to kneel at the altar-rails and participate in the sacred rite which, in the long-gone days, her little Claude-Marie had loved to serve. Never any more would she hear the rise and fall of the glorious plain chant under the grey arches; never more would she take part in fast or feast.

"I have loved, O Lord, the beauty of Thy house, the place where Thy glory dwelleth!" Well could the Mère Gilette say that, and now she was to have her reward. She was to enter into the courts of the Lord's house, to dwell there for evermore. She had loved to listen to the great organ rolling forth the solemn chants—it was never desecrated with the florid music which English choirs delight to indulge in—but she would hear it no more on earth. When next the sound of chanting broke on her ears it would be the chanting of the heavenly choirs, and she would hear, as in the days of old, her little Claude-Marie sing, "Hosanna to the Lord of life, Hosanna, Hosanna to the King."

And when M. le Curé had gone, there followed what so often follows the administration of the last sacraments—for the Mère Gilette had been anointed while the miners were being paid: the sick woman's eyes closed and she slept calmly, peacefully. All through the long dark hours of the winter's night, while the clock in the turret chimed quarter after quarter, Mère Gilette lay sleeping, and it was not till after half-past five, when in the sabbath stillness the bells began to peal for first Mass, that she opened her eyes.

"Time, time for church," she said faintly, and made as though she would rise.

"Not to-day, *mon amie*, not to-day," Madame de Mérillac said gently, and placed her hand upon the woman's shoulder.

"But it is Sunday—the feast of God—I must go. Holy Church requires it."

"But not when we are ill. *Mon amie*, the Church is our mother, she has care for the health of her children. You must lie still."

The Mère Gilette was quiet for a moment or two, then she began to moan. The remembrance of it all had come back to her, and again she strove to rise.

"I must go," she said, "I must go. It is not fitting that I should receive your kindness. *Mon Dieu*, that I should live to see the day on which my son should lead a mob against your house! I say, it is not fitting I should lie here. And Babette—I must see Babette. He—loved her—yes—yes—long ago he loved her. She was the only girl he ever cared for. If she could see him, she might lead him back to penitence. A woman may play the part of one of God's bright angels in a man's life. True she can, if evil, drag him down to Hell, but if she is good, she may raise him to the highest heights. It is a fearful power that which God has given to women, but praise be to Him, Babette is good. She loved my Jean —she loves him still—I am sure of it. Madame will forgive me, but he is my son. I cannot, nay, though he has done this cruel wrong to you, I cannot spurn him. Madame knows—she has been a mother—only those who have had children of their own know what it is—the heart of a mother."

"I know," Madame de Mérillac answered, and she looked at Jean and smiled. He was standing at the head of the bed. The Mère Gilette could not see him, could not see that the broad shoulders shook as he strove to subdue the emotion which the sound of his mother's voice aroused in him. Madame de Mérillac waved him back when he would have come out and shown himself. She feared to agitate the old woman. He must wait, she whispered, till the doctor came and gave him leave.

"If I could see Babette," Mère Gilette murmured. "Perhaps, Madame is so good, she would not mind sending for her."

Madame de Mérillac smiled. "Is there anything, *mon amie*, that you could ask that I would not try to do? Listen, it is very early yet; by and by Babette will go to church. Always on Sundays and feasts I see her at the seven o'clock Mass. Now, if you will close your eyes and try to sleep, I myself will hear that Mass, and I will bring her back with me. But you must promise me to try and sleep."

The old woman smiled her thanks and closed her eyes, and by and by the heavy breathing told that she had fulfilled her late mistress' request. Madame de Mérillac rose, and leaving the maid to watch the patient, signed to Jean to follow her.

The faint, grey light of dawn was visible in the long, deserted corridor when the young man and the lady of the house emerged from the sick-room, and softly closed the door behind them. Sending her companion to lie down, and giving him strict orders that he was not to stir till he was called, Madame de Mérillac, having wrapped herself in her warmest shawl, made her way under the bare trees to the church. As she passed up the Norman nave, she saw Babette kneeling on her chair, her eyes gazing up at the altar. The candles were lighted, and M. le Curé in his violet vestment was arranging the chalice as Madame de Mérillac took her accustomed place, and opened her big prayer-book.

Introibo ad altare Dei:
Ad Deum qui lætificat juventutem meam.

The low murmur of the voices of the priest and server was the only sound that broke the stillness, save the occasional tinkle of a bell at one or other of the side-altars where other Masses were being said. Madame de Mérillac bowed her head and clasped her hands as she prayed for her old friend and servant, and asked that comfort might be brought to the heart of the dying woman, while Babette, poor, gentle Babette, gazed up at the crucifix, and wiped away the tears that *would* come.

She was so sad, so tired. All the long, black winter's night she had lain awake, thinking of the dreadful news which her father had brought in at supper-time; how Jean, her own Jean, had led the attack on the *château*. It was terrible! She could not, would not believe it. And yet M. Rison had been positive, had called him a scoundrel, a knave, and every other sort of hard name. And after the sleepless night, Babette had come to the grey, dusky church, and striven to pray, and failed. There are such moments in all our lives, when one is too sick and faint and broken to pray, when one can only, as it were, lay one's heart before God, and remind Him that it is there and leave everything to Him. So that Advent Sunday morning Babette did not pray, only gazed up at the white Christ and the golden chalice, and now and then signed herself with the holy sign.

"Babette!"

Madame de Mérillac called the girl, as, in the early winter's morning, they stepped out into the clear air when Mass was over, and M. le Curé had disappeared within the sacristy. The December sun was shining down on the little town, making the roofs of the houses, covered with the white snow, flash and glitter as though encrusted with jewels. It was very beautiful out there, in the presence of the great king of day.

"Babette!"

The girl stopped.

"Madame called?" she asked.

"Yes; I want you to come with me to the *château*—to come with me to see some one, Babette, who is going away upon a great journey—going away to where those she loved have gone many years ago."

Babette did not answer. Her face had grown very pale while Madame de Mérillac had been speaking, but when the latter came to the words, "those she loved," the girl gave a little gasp of relief. It was not Jean—not Jean, with all his faults—who was going, but some one else. The hazel eyes looked up inquiringly at Madame de Mérillac.

"It is Mère Gilette who is passing away from among us," she said in answer. "Yesterday she had a stroke. There is no pain—at least no bodily pain."

Babette did not answer. Alas! she knew who was the cause of that other pain—that pain not of the body, but of the heart, and yet, yet she loved him still, she could not help it. Sometimes it is thus. To forget! That is not easy always—at least, with some natures.

"It is perhaps best," Babette said with a sigh. "She has suffered so much! M. le Curé says, that when that is the case, *le bon Dieu* takes the soul swiftly through the cleansing fires." Then the girl's voice failed her, and she broke down.

For a few moments Madame de Mérillac let the girl's grief have full sway, then she took Babette's hand in hers and patted it softly.

"Come, come, *mon enfant*," she said. "Things are not so bad as they might be. This Jean is a fine fellow; he behaved well, nobly, yesterday. If it had not been for his bravery and determination the *château* would have been burnt over our heads. It was when he was coming to our aid that his poor mother saw him, and believed, as indeed I did at that time, that he was directing the attack. And, all the while, he had travelled, wounded as he had been by the mob earlier in the day, to aid us if there should be danger. He has told me all. His poor mother does not yet know. We feared to agitate her. Yes, he is certainly a fine fellow. Tell me, Babette, is it true what is said, that you have a warm corner for him still in that big heart of yours?"

Babette was silent. The head was bent, and the eyelids fell, and Madame la Duchesse could only guess that a hot blush had swept across the girl's countenance at her question. By and by the answer came.

"It is true," she said, hanging her head, "I do love him," and then, with sudden and greater determination, "I do love him—I do!"

Madame de Mérillac smiled. "I hope," she said, "that he will prove worthy of your love and that it may yet come right. I think myself that with good influence he may rise—nay, I am sure of it. He has been influenced by the counsels of evil men. When we are young, that is a thing that is likely to happen. His poor mother will rejoice. I shall leave it to you, Babette, to tell her the good news—that we have been mistaken, that Jean was but coming to our aid, and that all was subsequently owed to him. If the doctor gives us leave, Babette shall tell the tale," and once again Madame de Mérillac patted the girl's hand.

"O, I am so glad, so happy," Babette answered. "My father believed also that it was Jean who brought the men. All the night I could not sleep because of what he told me, and it is all a mistake, and then to hear you say what you have said, Madame! If it were not for poor Mère Gilette, I should be so happy."

The turret-clock was chiming the quarter after

eight, when Madame la Duchesse and her companion reached the front door. The doctor's gig was standing waiting, and on the steps was the little man himself. He made a low bow.

"I have seen my patient," he said; "I was only waiting to see Madame to make my report. I have brought some drugs and given directions, but Madame la Duchesse will understand, drugs are but of little avail. I do not think she will rally. If she has aught to arrange, now is the hour. Before evening she will be at rest—at least I think so. I will come again, later in the day, should Madame wish, or if my presence can be of any comfort, but for the present I will go on my way."

Madame de Mérillac thanked the little man, and asked that he would return in the afternoon.

"Are you busy, Monsieur, this morning?" she asked.

"No, Madame, only one or two places. I start always early on the mornings of Sundays and *fêtes*, so that I may be present at the *Grande Messe* with my good sister who keeps my house for me. Madame is aware it is at Mass that one gains strength for the week's work."

Then he bowed, and entered his gig and drove away through the sunlight and the glittering snow.

It was quiet in the sick-room: no sound but the hiss of the smouldering logs on the hearth, and the laboured breathing of the dying woman. The closing of the door caused her to open her eyes. She looked up and saw Babette.

"My child," she said, "it is the good God Who has sent you to visit me. I want you to do something for me if you will. Look you, my child, my poor boy has done wrong—before, had he returned, they would have looked coldly on him, but now! now that he has done this, who will say a word for him? In the old days, Babette, he loved you. Your heart has not quite closed to him yet, I think. Perhaps if you were to be gentle to him, to speak a friendly word now and then, should he remain here, it might save him. I cannot ask more. It would be selfish to hope that he might yet win you. Say, my child, that you will be good to him, that when others turn their backs on him, you will not? It will comfort my dying hours if you say that it shall be so. I know that in the days of old your influence over him was for good. Often when the clouds of discontent were first settling on him, if he had seen you he would come back his old self, bright and cheerful. Ah, if he had been able to marry you then all this misery would never have happened. Now his chance is over; your father would not consent after this. And besides, even in the old days, it was not really fitting. Your father is rich, his position is above ours. For generations the Risons have held the old farm, and my poor Jean was but honest Turquin's apprentice."

"It would not have mattered. My father can dower me. What does the other matter as long as one cares———. When first we were betrothed, he said I was too young, and that he must first see that Jean could work well and was capable of rising. That was all he wanted."

The Mère Gilette sighed. "Ah, well, that is over now," she said, "but Babette, you will be good to him now that I, his mother, am leaving him—you will say now and again the kindly word? If I had lived, I might have saved him. The heart of a mother is open always to her child."

"But why should people turn against him?" Babette asked with a little light of pride coming into her eyes. "Listen—they have let me tell you—it is all a mistake. The miners had wounded Jean, and it was to save us all from danger that he came all those miles, it was he who offered his life to save the *château*. There was some mistake about money, I do not understand it quite, it had to do with the strike, and they were angry with Jean because some wicked man in Paris had run away with it, and so he told them that if they would spare the *château* he would come down and deliver himself up into their hands. Madame la Duchesse has said he was brave as a lion. It was Madame who would not let him throw his life away to save her house. It was all a mistake. Ah, if you had known, you need not have been ill!"

Babette ceased to speak, and the Mère Gilette lay speechless. She could not realize all at once what had been told her. She had been smitten down by the evil doings of her son, and lo! there had been no evil doings after all. The Lord God Almighty had stretched forth His hand to her and delivered her in her hour of need. She had striven to serve Him all her life, and His promise never to desert those who do so had been fulfilled to the very letter. Surely the Mother of Sorrows must have made intercession for her! She could not, I say, realize it at first. It seemed too good, too perfect to be true. By and by her lips moved a little.

"Blessed be God," she said, "Blessed be God, Who hath done great things for me. It is well, it is well, I am content. Bring me my son, that I may kiss him ere I die."

And so Babette went out into the corridor in

search of Jean, and found him sitting in one of the deep window-sills near the door of the room where his mother lay. His head was resting on his hands, and he did not hear the girl's soft tread; it was only when she spoke his name that he looked up with a start of amazement and saw her, saw her with her brown-gold hair, and her tall graceful form, and her gentle smile.

"Jean," she said, just as though nothing had ever happened, ever come between them, "thy good mother would see thee."

He rose and stood before her as she spoke. He could not answer. To see her standing there, calling him by his name, to see her unchanged, just as she was in the days of old, just as she had so often come back to him in his dreams, struck him dumb. He could only gaze at her as at some vision. He loved her, never till the day he left her did he know how dearly, and from that hour his love seemed to increase, and he had longed for a glimpse of the figure he knew so well, the figure in the black serge dress with the white kerchief folded across her breast, which was standing in front of him in the hush of the Sabbath stillness.

"You will come to her, will you not?" Babette said, looking up. "She is very ill. I have told her all, how it was a mistake, and how nobly you offered your life. O, it has made her so glad! I think that now she will die quite happy. Come, she is waiting," and she put out her hand to lead him to the room.

For a moment Jean hesitated. He thought of the days in Paris, of the vile, painted women among whom he had lived, and he felt unworthy to touch the hand of this young and innocent girl. Then as a little look of disappointment came upon her face, he stretched forth his own rough hand and it was clasped in Babette's.

And hand in hand in silence they passed to the door of the sick-room. Then the girl drew back.

"She will like best to have you all to herself, at least for a while," she said.

Jean did not answer for a moment, then he said: "You have given me back what I have lost, my faith. It is *le bon Dieu* Whom I have doubted, Who has made you what you are." Then he turned and entered the room.

And so no one but God and His holy angels saw the meeting of the mother and son. Only in the hush, Babette could hear the deep sobs of Jean, and the low murmur of the Mère Gilette's voice in the canticle of holy Simeon: *Nunc dimittis servum tuum, Domine : secundum verbum tuum in pace.*

"It is well," Madame de Mérillac said, when a little before noon she returned from *Grande Messe*, and Babette, meeting her in the hall, told her that the mother and son were alone together. "It is well. We will leave them so. The hours are short which are left. They are precious moments, these; he will live on them for years," and she sat silent, thinking of the dying hours of her child.

The time wore on. The bells had pealed, and vespers were over, the sermon preached, and M. le Curé was laying aside his muslin surplice in the sacristy, through the little windows of which came the last rays of the dying winter sun, when a messenger from the *château* came bidding him come in haste if he would see the Mère Gilette again. It was almost dark when he entered the still chamber, only lighted by a single wax taper, which seemed if possible to increase the gloom. The eyes of the dying woman were closed, but she opened them a little when the priest pronounced the last absolution over her, and gave a little smile, as though of thanks. Then she rested her right hand on the head of her son, and then on that of Babette.

"The Lord bless thee," she said to each.

They were the last words she ever spoke.

When, in the hush of the death-chamber, M.

le Curé reached the words in the commendatory prayer, *Proficiscere, anima Christiana, de hoc mundo*—" Go forth, O Christian soul, from this world," there was just a little sigh, and it was over.

"She was always obedient," M. le Curé said with one of his slow, sad smiles. Then he covered his face with his hands, and knelt far into the night beside the dead body of the woman, whose soul he had tended through many years on its upward path to Heaven.

A day or two afterwards, just before the great feast of Christmas, they bore the Mère Gilette up the steep little Grande Rue, past the cottage with its closed shutters, and in through those wooden gates to the place where her husband, and the children, whom the Lord had given her, lay resting in the serene repose of death. The solemn words of the ritual were spoken, and the angel guard besought to watch that place of sepulchre, and then in the twilight hour they turned away, and left her lying there in peace, with God's soft rain falling gently on the earth and tangled grass.

"Come back to the *château*, Jean," Madame de Mérillac, said, when on their return the procession broke up; but the young man would not.

"I thank you, Madame," he said, "but just now I am best alone," and he went away to the deserted cottage, which in the days of old his mother's hands had kept so spick and span. Those hands were folded across her breast now, and work was done, Jean thought, and then his eyes fell on the wisps of dusty corn, and he thought of the meeting between her and little Claude-Marie, and relief came in a burst of tears.

"Thy place waits for thee, friend," honest Turquin said the next morning, entering the little cottage. "If thou thinkest it worth while to return, right gladly will I bid thee welcome," and then the rough hand wiped away a tear which had gathered in the handsome grey eyes of the blacksmith, for he had looked round the little room, and it brought back his old friend, the Mère Gilette.

"If you will receive me, I will come," Jean said, and Turquin looked at him. The great blacksmith's nature was tender. The memory of his own mother lived yet fresh in his kindly heart.

"Once it was so with me," he said, and took the arm of his apprentice, and went with him to the forge.

And through the winter's day Jean sat at work,

and heard once again the bellows roar, and the water lapping against the bridge, as in the days of old, only at night when he went home, the little place was very still—very still. There was no fire on the hearth. He had to kindle that himself. The hands that once had done it for him so lovingly were at rest for evermore.

Christmas came, and on the eve of the feast, in the great dusky Norman church, Jean knelt in the confessional of M. le Curé, and the next morning knelt near Babette to receive the Bread of the Strong. And the bells pealed, and the organ gave forth its solemn chants, and Jean's thoughts were with those who kept the feast on high.

The days rolled by. Jean hoped each day for a sight of Babette, but, except at Mass on Sundays, he never saw her now. Every day he seemed to grow more sad and wretched and lonely.

"Is there no hope for thee any longer with thy sweetheart?" Turquin asked one spring day, when Jean had refused to take a holiday which his master thought would be good for him. "Is there no hope?"

"I do not think so—it is my past life, I suppose," Jean answered.

Turquin was vexed, and questioned M. le Curé.

"It is M. Rison," the priest answered. "He will not hear of it. Babette will have a large dower. It is not a fitting match. And then, too, he is afraid of the young man's past."

The blacksmith went away and sat silent for the rest of the day thinking, thinking. That evening after supper, he asked his Fanchette whether she did not think it time that he gave up work. They had no children—they were well-to-do. For his part, he should be glad to rest. Then he waited, rather frightened. Fanchette was a good wife, though a little inclined to tyrannize at times, but she loved her husband for all that, and she saw what he was driving at. She went across, and sat beside him.

"It is true we are rich, but that you wish to rest, I do not believe. I know that you love the old forge, and the work, and the gossip, and the rest of it, but you think if you gave it up to young Gilette, M. Rison would consent to his daughter's marriage. Is that not so?"

Fanchette was a wonderful woman. Turquin had often said so before, and now he said it again.

"It is a noble and kindly thought, husband," she said. "And if you carry it out, I will seek to make your home and your leisure happy. Perhaps sometimes in the past I have been a little quick."

Turquin kissed his wife and declared that in all Normandy no man had a happier home than he. The next day he made the proposal to M. Rison. The farmer would not hear of it. He feared the young man's steadfastness.

"If you should alter, remember I stand to my offer still," Turquin said, and went back down the lane and across the bridge to the forge, and the work he loved.

The days went on. Jean worked harder, and grew, if possible, more sad and lonely. He would see no one. He thanked all who asked him, but he was best alone, he said. Every evening at dusk, he went to the cemetery, and knelt by his mother's grave. And there one evening, when many days had come and gone, M. Rison, visiting his own wife's grave, found him. He bent down and touched the young man's shoulder.

"Poor fellow," he said; "you have suffered much. It was my duty to wait and watch. Jean, if I give you my girl, you will be good to her?"

"I will," the other answered simply, but M. Rison was satisfied.

That night, Jean supped in the old oak kitchen of the farm, and feasted his eyes on Babette, who blushed crimson every time she caught his glance. And when it was time to go she went with him to the gate. The latch was difficult to unfasten, she said, and M. Rison smiled, and did not offer to accompany his guest. And the air was soft and sweet, and the latch took a wonderful while to unfasten, and the pale moon looked down on the young lovers standing there just as through hundreds of years she has so often done before. Jean went away a very happy man that night.

And the next day, Turquin told him that he was for the future master of the forge, and Madame de Mérillac came herself to congratulate him, and to tell him that she would give Babette her wedding-dress. And then M. le Curé came, and walked up the hill, and spoke of God's goodness, and the heart of Jean felt full.

One bright autumn day, the church bells pealed, and Jean and Babette were wed, and the kind faces of friends gazed on them as they knelt; and the days of Paris and the evil hours spent there seemed like some ugly dream, Jean thought. And then M. le Curé drew near with the great golden ciborium, and bride and bridegroom received Him Who, long years ago, deigned to bless a marriage-feast in far-off Cana of Galilee.

"I think of thy good mother this day," Madame de Mérillac said as she shook hands with the pair in the old porch.

"And so do I," Babette said, and looked at her husband, but Jean was silent—he could not speak.

But as they stood silent with the golden sunshine falling all about them, M. le Curé, who had heard the last words, spoke:

"'The souls of the just are in the hand of God, and the torment of death shall not touch them. In the sight of the unwise they seemed to die and their departure was taken for misery, and their going away from us, utter destruction, but they are in peace. As gold in the furnace He hath proved them, and as a victim of a holocaust He hath received them, and in time there shall be respect had to them.' I think Jean should be a proud man this day, for it seemeth to me that the words of Holy Writ are fulfilled here, in the esteem felt by you all for the memory of Mère Gilette."

For an instant, as the hushed tones of the priest ceased, there was a silence, broken only by the soft pealing of the bells above, and then there came from the throng a murmur as though they said among themselves that he—this Curé—had spoken well and truly. Perchance so it was.

THE END.

www.ingramcontent.com/pod-product-compliance
Lightning Source LLC
Chambersburg PA
CBHW020934230426
43666CB00008B/1669